UNDERSTANDING THE SIDDUR II

SPECIAL READINGS THROUGH THE JEWISH YEAR

UNDERSTANDING THE SIDDUR II

SPECIAL READINGS THROUGH THE JEWISH YEAR

by

Carl S. Ehrlich and Michal Shekel

KTAV PUBLISHING HOUSE, INC.

HOBOKEN, NEW JERSEY

FOR OUR PARENTS:
EDITH AND LEONARD EHRLICH
TAMAR AND JACOB SHEKEL

TABLE OF CONTENTS

TO THE TEACHER

This book is meant as a sequel to *Understanding the Siddur I* by Shirley Stern. Stern's book serves to give the somewhat advanced religious school student of Hebrew an appreciation of the structure, concepts, and language of the basic Jewish liturgy. In addition, *Understanding the Siddur I* includes sections devoted to some of the major prayers for special events in the Jewish calendar.

Although there have been a number of books devoted to the standard Jewish liturgy, this book attempts to fill a void in the curriculum of the Jewish school by devoting a full course of study to the cycle of prayers and special readings that one is apt to encounter during the Jewish year. From the Mahzor to the Megillot, *Understanding the Siddur II* not only teaches the students the *peshat* of these readings, but also teaches about the readings in a way that should be both interesting and stimulating.

In addition to Hebrew curriculums, this book can be utilized in liturgy, prayer, and holiday curriculums. The choice of readings and their presentation have been geared to Conservative religious schools.

All translations are the authors' own. The attempt has been made to render the Hebrew in readable English translations, which are as close as idiomatically possible to the original Hebrew. In their writing, the authors have endeavored to avoid sexist language. However, since this book will serve some students as a vehicle for learning the Hebrew language, it was decided not to mistranslate the Hebrew in order to render the English more acceptable to our modern ears. It is strongly suggested that teachers spend time with their classes dealing with the issue of ancient texts and modern sensibilities. The students should be made aware that human thought is an evolving process. This applies no more and no less to the process of Jewish thought.

The authors would like to thank Sol Scharfstein and Howard Adelman of Ktav Publishing House, who saw this project through to its completion. We would also like to thank Rabbi Stephen D. Franklin of the Riverdale Temple for his invaluable help.

In dedicating this book to our respective sets of parents, we are acknowledging a priceless inheritance.

In their treatment of the Tetragrammaton, the four letter name of God, the authors have avoided the standard translation as "Lord." Instead, we have provided a transcription of the Hebrew euphemism for the Name, i.e. "Adonai."

C.S.E.
M.S.

ABOUT THE AUTHORS

CARL S. EHRLICH is in the process of completing a Ph.D. in Biblical Studies at Harvard University. While writing his dissertation, he is serving as the Educational Director of the Riverdale Temple in the Bronx. He holds a B.A. in Judaic Studies from the University of Massachusetts at Amherst and has done graduate work and excavated extensively in Israel.

MICHAL SHEKEL is one of the first women to study for the rabbinate at the Jewish Theological Seminary of America. She holds a B.A. from the University of Massachusetts at Amherst in the field of Anthropology, and an M.S. in Communications from Boston University. She has also authored the workbook and the teacher's guide for *All About Israel* for Ktav.

While writing this book, Michal and Carl celebrated the birth of their first child, Joseph Emanuel.

TO THE STUDENT

By now you are probably quite familiar with the order of the synagogue service and with the prayers that are most frequently recited there. Instead of taking you step-by-step through the service, this book will take you on a journey through the Jewish year. This book is about the special readings that are associated with the passage of the year.

Although you would probably agree with Kohelet (about whom you will learn in the following pages) that "there is no end to making books, and too much studying is tiring," we hope that you will find material of interest in this book, and that it will help you attain an added appreciation for a collection of Jewish literature you may have not have thought about too much in the past. Shanah Tovah! Have a good year!

SELICHOT סְלִיחוֹת
APPROACHING THE NEW YEAR

Everyone knows that the Jewish New Year begins on Rosh Hashanah, the first day of the Jewish month of Tishri. We all know that Rosh Hashanah and Yom Kippur are the holidays during which we ask to be forgiven for the wrongs we have committed in the past year. Yet this cycle of asking for forgiveness actually begins *before* the start of the Jewish year.

Selichot prayers are prayers asking for forgiveness that are recited at different times of the year. The most familiar ones are said before Rosh Hashanah. These prayers are intended to prepare us for the solemn days ahead, the *Yamim Nora'im*, the Ten Days of Awe from Rosh Hashanah to Yom Kippur. Many of the prayers recited at this service will be repeated again during Rosh Hashanah and Yom Kippur.

Traditionally, Selichot prayers are said at midnight of the Shabbat right before Rosh Hashanah. Because these services take place at the end of Shabbat, many congregations begin with *Havdalah*, the short service that ends Shabbat. The Selichot service itself focuses on God as the divine judge and asks God to forgive us for our wrongdoings. We begin by reminding God that we are at this service at an unusual time—after Shabbat—and we are here for a special purpose.

FROM THE SELICHOT INTRODUCTION

At the end of the Sabbath,	בְּמוֹצָאֵי מְנוּחָה,
as we begin to approach you,	קִדַּמְנוּךְ תְּחִלָּה,
Incline your ear from on high,	הַט אָזְנְךָ מִמָּרוֹם,
dweller in Glory,	יוֹשֵׁב תְּהִלָּה,
To listen to [our] song and prayer.	לִשְׁמוֹעַ אֶל הָרִנָּה וְאֶל הַתְּפִלָּה.

Before asking for forgiveness, we remind ourselves that God is a merciful judge, and we remind God that he deals kindly with his creations.

10

Adonai, Adonai	יְהוָֹה יְהוָֹה.
is a compassionate and merciful God,	אֵל רַחוּם וְחַנּוּן,
Slow to anger,	אֶרֶךְ אַפַּיִם,
abundant in goodness and truth,	וְרַב חֶסֶד וֶאֱמֶת,
Preserving kindness	נֹצֵר חֶסֶד
for thousands [of generations],	לָאֲלָפִים
Forgiving evil, wickedness,	נֹשֵׂא עָוֹן וָפֶשַׁע
and sin, and pardoning.	וְחַטָּאָה וְנַקֵּה.

ASKING FOR FORGIVENESS

This reminder of God's kindness gives us the courage to make a request. We ask God to forgive us and to have mercy on us:

Listen to our voice, Adonai our God.	שְׁמַע קוֹלֵנוּ, יְהוָֹה, אֱלֹהֵינוּ
Have compassion upon us and be merciful.	חוּס וְרַחֵם עָלֵינוּ.
Accept our prayer with compassion and goodwill.	וְקַבֵּל בְּרַחֲמִים וּבְרָצוֹן אֶת תְּפִלָּתֵנוּ.
Restore us, Adonai,	הֲשִׁיבֵנוּ, יְהוָֹה אֵלֶיךָ,
and we shall be restored,	וְנָשׁוּבָה,
Renew our days as of old.	חַדֵּשׁ יָמֵינוּ כְּקֶדֶם.

(These last three lines are a direct quotation from the Book of Eicha/Lamentations, which is discussed in the chapter on Tisha B'Av.)

PRAYER VOCABULARY

your ear	אָזְנְךָ	forgiving	נֹשֵׂא
song	רִנָּה	our voice	קוֹלֵנוּ
prayer	תְּפִלָּה	our prayer	תְּפִלָּתֵנוּ
compassionate	רַחוּם	our days	יָמֵינוּ
merciful	וְחַנּוּן		

Only now do we confess the wrongdoing for which we wish to be forgiven. Since this prayer is said by the entire congregation, each person confesses to many things that he or she has not personally committed. The idea of the confession is to stand united as a group and to be judged as a group. The confession is repeated many times in different forms from Selichot until the end of Yom Kippur. In reciting the confession, each Jew is asking forgiveness not just for him or herself, but for everyone else.

Our God, and God of our ancestors:	אֱלֹהֵינוּ, וֵאלֹהֵי אֲבוֹתֵינוּ:
May our prayer come before you,	תָּבֹא לְפָנֶיךָ תְּפִלָּתֵנוּ,
and do not hide from our supplication!	וְאַל תִּתְעַלַּם מִתְּחִנָּתֵנוּ!
We are not so insolent or arrogant	שֶׁאֵין אָנוּ עַזֵּי פָנִים וּקְשֵׁי עוֹרֶף
as to claim before you,	לוֹמַר לְפָנֶיךָ
"Adonai our God,	"יְהֹוָה אֱלֹהֵינוּ,
and God of our ancestors,	וֵאלֹהֵי אֲבוֹתֵינוּ,
we are righteous and have not sinned."	צַדִּיקִים אֲנַחְנוּ וְלֹא חָטָאנוּ".
But we have indeed sinned.	אֲבָל, אֲנַחְנוּ חָטָאנוּ.

Focus on Asking Forgiveness

Originally, Selichot prayers were not said at just one time of year. These special prayers were regularly recited in times of trouble. The Talmud mentions special prayers for drought. In the Middle Ages, special fast-days that used Selichot prayers were called during times of persecution. Jews believed that since God is just, any bad incident that happened to the Jewish community was because the community had sinned. Therefore, the only way to improve conditions was by repenting as a community. This was done through fasting and praying for forgiveness through the Selichot prayers. Fasting and praying are still the major Jewish symbols of repenting for wrongdoing. After all, Yom Kippur, the Day of Atonement, is devoted solely to these activites.

After confessing to all the wrongdoings that the community may have committed, we are worried that the judgment which we deserve will be harsh. We therefore remind God of his special relationship with the Jewish people:

O Guardian of Israel,	שׁוֹמֵר יִשְׂרָאֵל.
guard the remnant of Israel!	שְׁמוֹר שְׁאֵרִית יִשְׂרָאֵל.
May the Jews not perish, they who recite	וְאַל יֹאבַד יִשְׂרָאֵל הָאוֹמְרִים:
the Shema Israel!	"שְׁמַע יִשְׂרָאֵל."

Finally, having acknowledged the divine judge, confessed our wrongdoing, and reminded God of his mercy, we ask to be forgiven:

Our Father, our King,	אָבִינוּ, מַלְכֵּנוּ,
be gracious unto us and answer us.	חָנֵּנוּ וַעֲנֵנוּ,
for we have no merit [deeds].	כִּי אֵין בָּנוּ מַעֲשִׂים.
Deal with us justly and mercifully,	עֲשֵׂה עִמָּנוּ צְדָקָה וָחֶסֶד,
and save us.	וְהוֹשִׁיעֵנוּ.

The Selichot service is very short, but the ideas in it are powerful. These same ideas, which employ the same expressions over and over again, are repeated on both Rosh Hashanah and Yom Kippur. Selichot acts as a dress rehearsal, preparing us for the mood of the Yamim Nora'im, the Days of Awe, which begin on the first of Tishri with Rosh Hashanah.

PRAYER VOCABULARY

insolent	עַזֵּי פָנִים	our King	מַלְכֵּנוּ
arrogant	וּקְשֵׁי עוֹרֶף	be gracious unto us	חָנֵּנוּ
our ancestors	אֲבוֹתֵינוּ	and answer us	וַעֲנֵנוּ
guardian	שׁוֹמֵר	and save us	וְהוֹשִׁיעֵנוּ
remnant	שְׁאֵרִית		

יָמִים נוֹרָאִים
YAMIM NORA'IM:
THE DAYS OF AWE

NEW YEAR

Rosh Hashanah, the Jewish New Year, begins on the first day of the month of *Tishri*. But the Jewish New Year is not a noisy "happy new year" celebration like the first of January. In the Talmud it is written that Tishri is the appropriate time of year to ask for repentance and forgiveness.

According to Jewish tradition, the Book of Life is opened on Rosh Hashanah. The book is sealed ten days later on Yom Kippur. During the first ten days of Tishri, it is still possible to make changes in the Book of Life. During these ten days, Jews have one final chance to atone for all the bad deeds they may have committed during the past year. These ten days are known as the Yamim Nora'im, the Days of Awe. It is a very solemn period of time, when every Jew is considered to be awaiting judgment.

In order to help all Jews receive the best judgment possible—another year of life, prayers of repentance are said throughout this ten-day period. These prayers are found in a special book called the Mahzor.

In their prayers throughout the year, Jews use a prayerbook called the *Siddur*. The word *Siddur* is Hebrew and means "order." Ever since Siddurim have been compiled, there have been differences among them. Ashkenazi and Sephardi Jews use different Siddurim. Jews in Israel do not use the same Siddur as Jews elsewhere in the world. In the United States, Orthodox, Conservative, Reform, and Reconstructionist Jews each use a different Siddur. Some of these Siddurim even have special names. For example, the Reform Siddur is called *Gates of Prayer* שַׁעֲרֵי תְּפִלָּה. The old reform siddur is called the *Union Prayer Book.* The Siddur put out by the Conservative Rabbinical Assembly is called the Silverman *Sabbath and Festival Prayer Book.* The Conservative movement has also published a new Siddur called *Siddur Sim Shalom* סִדּוּר שִׂים שָׁלוֹם. What all Siddurim have in common is that they contain prayers and services for the weekday, Shabbat, and festivals.

At certain times of the year, a special prayerbook is needed, because on certain holy days, the prayers recited differ greatly from the weekly prayers. During the holidays associated with the new year, a prayerbook called the Mahzor is used.

Mahzor is a Hebrew word meaning "cycle." It is used for a special cycle of holy days. Historically, there were many different Mahzorim for the Jewish holidays throughout the year. In modern times, the prayerbook called the Mahzor is used for the High Holy Days—Rosh Hashanah and Yom Kippur. Just like the Siddur, the Mahzor may vary among the different groups of Jews. Conservative Jews refer to their Mahzor as the Silverman *High Holiday Prayerbook.* The new Conservative Mahzor is called *Mahzor for Rosh Hashanah and Yom Kippur, edited by Rabbi Jules Harlow.*

PRAYER VOCABULARY

Days of Awe	יָמִים נוֹרָאִים	**Rosh Hashanah**	רֹאשׁ הַשָּׁנָה
Mahzor—Holiday Prayerbook	מַחֲזוֹר	**fast**	צוֹם
		Day of Atonement	יוֹם כִּפּוּר

THE MAHZOR AND THE SIDDUR

In many ways, the Mahzor is similar to the Siddur. It too contains prayers that are to be said at the three times a day that Jews traditionally pray. Because the Mahzor is used on a holiday, it contains an additional morning service called *Musaf*, "additional service," just as the traditional Siddur has a Musaf service for Shabbat.

THE PRAYERS OF THE DAYS OF AWE

What makes the Mahzor different is that, in concentrating on prayers for Rosh Hashanah and Yom Kippur, it conveys a different attitude than the normal Siddur. Sometimes this is done by adding words to prayers already found in the Siddur. For instance, in the silent prayer, the Amidah, we find these additions:

Who is like you, merciful Father,	מִי כָמוֹךָ אַב הָרַחֲמִים,
who remembers his creatures	זוֹכֵר יְצוּרָיו
for life in mercy?	לַחַיִּים בְּרַחֲמִים.

and:

Inscribe for a good life	וַחֲתוֹם לְחַיִּים טוֹבִים
all the children of your covenant.	כָּל־בְּנֵי בְרִיתֶךָ.

These two additions reveal a certain attitude shared by Jews during the High Holy Days. This is a special time, when certain requests are made of God. The Mahzor focuses on these requests: the wish for a good life, and the asking for mercy. During the High Holy Days, God is addressed not just as *Elohim* (God), but as the supreme ruler and judge, *melech*. Throughout the Mahzor, the prevailing feeling is that this is the time of judgment. During the High Holy Days, God, acting as judge and ruler, will decide every person's fate for the coming year.

On Rosh Hashanah [the judgment] is
    written,
    and on the fast of Yom Kippur it is
    sealed.

בְּרֹאשׁ הַשָּׁנָה
יִכָּתֵבוּן,
וּבְיוֹם צוֹם כִּפּוּר
יֵחָתֵמוּן.

But each person also has a chance to influence the final decision:

Repentance, prayer, and righteousness
    do away with the severe decree.

וּתְשׁוּבָה וּתְפִלָּה וּצְדָקָה
מַעֲבִירִין אֶת־רוֹעַ הַגְּזֵרָה.

The ultimate purpose of the Mahzor is to help each person improve and avoid a severe decree. That is why the Mahzor contains so many confessions of wrongdoing and pleas for mercy all addressed to the ultimate judge and ruler. The Mahzor is a prayerbook specifically designed for the needs of Jews on Rosh Hashanah and Yom Kippur.

PRAYER VOCABULARY

like you	כָּמוֹךְ	is written	יִכָּתֵבוּן
his creatures	יְצוּרָיו	it is sealed	יֵחָתֵמוּן
inscribe	חֲתוֹם	repentance	תְּשׁוּבָה
your covenant	בְּרִיתֶךָ	the severe decree	אֶת־רוֹעַ הַגְּזֵרָה

רֹאשׁ הַשָּׁנָה
ROSH HASHANAH:
THE NEW YEAR STARTS

Rosh Hashanah means "the beginning of the year." It is a holiday celebrated on the first day of the Jewish month of Tishri. Some Jews celebrate it for one day, others for two. According to Jewish tradition, the Book of Life is opened on Rosh Hashanah. Starting on Rosh Hashanah, and continuing for the next ten days, Jews try symbolically to get their names sealed for a good year in the Book of Life.

NEW YEAR CUSTOMS

Many Rosh Hashanah customs focus on the value of life. A round challah is eaten to symbolize the eternity of life. Apples are dipped in honey as a symbolic hope for a sweet life in the coming year.

THE KIDDUSH

As on other special days, such as Shabbat, the Kiddush over wine is recited on Rosh Hashanah. This blessing over wine is said either at home or at the synagogue. It begins in the same manner as on Shabbat:

BLESSING ON THE WINE

Blessed are you, Adonai our God,

    Ruler of the universe,

    Creator of the fruit of the vine.

בָּרוּךְ אַתָּה יְיָ,

אֱלֹהֵינוּ מֶלֶךְ הָעוֹלָם,

בּוֹרֵא פְּרִי הַגָּפֶן.

From this point on, the Kiddush differs from the Shabbat Kiddush. The rest of the Kiddush centers specifically on Rosh Hashanah, which is called Yom Hazikaron, the Day of Remembrance.

18

Blessed are you, Adonai our God,

    Ruler of the universe,

    who has chosen us from among all

      peoples

and exalted us above all tongues [people]

and hallowed us with his

      commandments.

בָּרוּךְ אַתָּה יְהֹוָה אֱלֹהֵינוּ,

מֶלֶךְ הָעוֹלָם,

אֲשֶׁר בָּחַר־בָּנוּ

מִכָּל־עָם

וְרוֹמְמָנוּ מִכָּל־לָשׁוֹן

וְקִדְּשָׁנוּ

בְּמִצְוֹתָיו.

You have given us, Adonai our God,

    with love, this (Shabbat

    and this) day of remembrance,

    this day of sounding the shofar

    (with love), a holy occasion

    recalling the Exodus from Egypt.

וַתִּתֶּן־לָנוּ יְהֹוָה אֱלֹהֵינוּ,

בְּאַהֲבָה אֶת [יוֹם הַשַּׁבָּת הַזֶּה

וְאֶת] יוֹם הַזִּכָּרוֹן הַזֶּה,

יוֹם תְּרוּעָה

[בְּאַהֲבָה] מִקְרָא קֹדֶשׁ

זֵכֶר לִיצִיאַת מִצְרָיִם.

You have chosen us and consecrated us

    from among all peoples.

כִּי בָנוּ בָחַרְתָּ וְאוֹתָנוּ קִדַּשְׁתָּ

מִכָּל־הָעַמִּים.

Your word is true, enduring forever.

וּדְבָרְךָ אֱמֶת וְקַיָּם לָעַד.

Blessed are you, Adonai,

    Ruler of all the world,

    who hallows (Shabbat

    and) Israel,

    and the day of remembrance.

בָּרוּךְ אַתָּה יְהֹוָה

מֶלֶךְ עַל כָּל־הָאָרֶץ

מְקַדֵּשׁ [הַשַּׁבָּת

וְ]יִשְׂרָאֵל

וְיוֹם הַזִּכָּרוֹן.

PRAYER VOCABULARY

day of remembrance	יוֹם הַזִּכָּרוֹן	you have chosen us	בָּנוּ בָחַרְתָּ
day of sounding the shofar	יוֹם תְּרוּעָה	who hallows	מְקַדֵּשׁ

A GOOD LIFE AND PEACE

The solemnity of Rosh Hashanah carries through for ten days until Yom Kippur. The same prayers are repeated throughout the services on these days. We ask to be inscribed for a good life.

In the book of life, blessing,	בְּסֵפֶר חַיִּים בְּרָכָה
peace, and prosperity	וְשָׁלוֹם וּפַרְנָסָה טוֹבָה
may we be remembered and inscribed	נִזָּכֵר וְנִכָּתֵם
before you,	לְפָנֶיךָ,
we and all your people	אֲנַחְנוּ וְכָל־עַמְּךָ
the house of Israel,	בֵּית יִשְׂרָאֵל,
for a good life and for peace.	לְחַיִּים טוֹבִים וּלְשָׁלוֹם.
Blessed are you, Adonai,	בָּרוּךְ אַתָּה יְיָ,
who makes peace.	עוֹשֵׂה הַשָּׁלוֹם.

AND FOR THE COMMUNITY

The wish for a good life and peace we ask not only for ourselves, but for everyone. Since Jewish tradition holds that the whole world is judged at this time of year, we ask for mercy for the entire community. On Rosh Hashanah, we begin asking for forgiveness for ourselves and for everyone else. These are requests that are meant to be repeated during the Yamim Nora'im. They are said for the final time each year during the services of Yom Kippur, when the Book of Life is closed and sealed for the year.

PRAYER VOCABULARY

Book of Life	בְּסֵפֶר חַיִּים	your people	עַמְּךָ
may we be remembered	נִזָּכֵר	house of Israel	בֵּית יִשְׂרָאֵל
and inscribed	וְנִכָּתֵם	for a good life	לְחַיִּים טוֹבִים

Focus on the New Year

The Bible tells us that the New Year begins in the month of Nissan, the month when we celebrate Passover. Yet Rosh Hashanah is celebrated half a year later at the beginning of Tishri! Actually, things get even more complicated than that. According to the rabbis there are four "new years" during the course of a single Jewish year. The first of Nissan was once considered the new year for Jewish rulers and for the cycle of Jewish festivals. The first of Elul was the new year for cattle, having to do with tithes (taxes) on animals. The first of Tishri was considered the new year according to the civil calendar. The first of Shevat was considered by some to be the new year of trees. How is it that Rosh Hashanah, *the* new year, ended up being celebrated on the first of Tishri? The Midrash says that the world was created in the autumn, in Tishri. Therefore, when we celebrate Rosh Hashanah, we are celebrating the beginning of all creation. Why is Rosh Hashanah such a solemn holiday? The Talmud says that on this day the whole world is judged.

קְרִיאַת הַתּוֹרָה לְרֹאשׁ הַשָּׁנָה
ROSH HASHANAH:
THE TORAH READINGS

The Torah readings for the two days of Rosh Hashanah are the twenty-first and twenty-second chapters of the Book of Genesis (Bereshit) respectively. In addition, on each day the first six verses of Numbers (Bamidbar) chapter 29 are read. This latter reading deals with the special sacrifices that used to be offered in the Temple on this holiday. In the Reform tradition, which often celebrates just one day of Rosh Hashanah, only Genesis 22 is read. The selections from Genesis deal with the beginning of the fulfillment of God's promises to Abraham, and with the extent of Abraham's faith in God.

THE BIRTH OF ISAAC: GENESIS 21:1–21

One of God's promises to Abraham was that he would make of Abraham's descendants a numerous and mighty people. However, Abraham's wife, Sarah, had been unable to conceive a child. Therefore, when she was well past child-bearing age, Abraham took a concubine, a secondary wife named Hagar, and had a son, Ishmael, by her.

ISAAC'S CONCEPTION

But God had not forgotten Sarah,

Adonai remembered Sarah as he had said,	וַיהֹוָה פָּקַד אֶת־שָׂרָה כַּאֲשֶׁר אָמָר,
and Adonai did for Sarah as he had foretold.	וַיַּעַשׂ יְהֹוָה לְשָׂרָה כַּאֲשֶׁר דִּבֵּר.

Sarah became pregnant and gave birth to a	וַתַּהַר וַתֵּלֶד שָׂרָה
son for Abraham	לְאַבְרָהָם
in his old age,	בֵּן לִזְקֻנָיו
at the time of year	לַמּוֹעֵד
which God had told him.	אֲשֶׁר־דִּבֶּר אֹתוֹ אֱלֹהִים.

ISAAC'S CIRCUMCISION

So Abraham named the son who was born to	וַיִּקְרָא אַבְרָהָם אֶת־שֶׁם־בְּנוֹ
him,	הַנּוֹלַד־לוֹ,
whom Sarah had borne for him, Isaac.	אֲשֶׁר־יָלְדָה־לּוֹ שָׂרָה יִצְחָק.
Abraham circumcised Isaac, his son,	וַיָּמָל אַבְרָהָם אֶת־יִצְחָק, בְּנוֹ,
on the eighth day,	בֶּן־שְׁמֹנַת יָמִים,
just as God had commanded him.	כַּאֲשֶׁר צִוָּה אֹתוֹ אֱלֹהִים.
Now Abraham was one hundred years old	וְאַבְרָהָם בֶּן־מְאַת שָׁנָה
when Isaac, his son, was born.	בְּהִוָּלֶד לוֹ אֵת יִצְחָק בְּנוֹ.
Then Sarah said,	וַתֹּאמֶר שָׂרָה
"God has brought me joy,	צְחֹק עָשָׂה לִי אֱלֹהִים
everyone who hears [of it] will rejoice	כָּל־הַשֹּׁמֵעַ יִצְחַק לִי."
with me."	[Gen 21:1–6]

Notice in this passage how the words *Isaac*, *joy*, and *rejoice* are all plays on the same root in Hebrew. In an earlier story, Sarah had "laughed" (וַתִּצְחַק) when she was told that she would still bear a child in her old age. Later, Isaac will be observed "playing" (מְצַחֵק) with his wife Rebecca. The Bible is filled with puns, which are clever plays on words.

PRAYER VOCABULARY			
and she gave birth	וַתֵּלֶד	his son	בְּנוֹ
in his old age	לִזְקֻנָיו	joy	צְחֹק
at the time of year	לַמּוֹעֵד	everyone who hears	הַשֹּׁמֵעַ
one hundred years old	בֶּן־מְאַת שָׁנָה	will rejoice	יִצְחַק

THE ARABS

Now that Abraham's wife, Sarah, had a child, she had Hagar and
Ishmael sent away, so that there would be no question of who
would receive the inheritance. God took Hagar and her son into
his care and promised Hagar that a mighty people would also be
descended from her son. According to tradition, the Arabs are the
descendants of Ishmael, while the Jews are the descendants of
Isaac. Thus, both peoples are descended from Abraham.

THE OATH AT BEER-SHEVA: GENESIS 21:22–34

The rest of chapter 21 tells the story of an oath sworn between
Abraham and Abimelech, one of the Philistine kings, at Beer-
Sheva in the Negev. Among other things, this story tells us how
Beer-Sheva got its name.

Abimelech asked Abraham,	וַיֹּאמֶר אֲבִימֶלֶךְ אֶל־אַבְרָהָם,
"What are these seven [*sheva*] lambs	„מָה הֵנָּה שֶׁבַע כְּבָשֹׂת הָאֵלֶּה
which you have set aside?"	אֲשֶׁר הִצַּבְתָּ לְבַדָּנָה?
He [Abraham] answered,	וַיֹּאמֶר,
"Take these seven [*sheva*] lambs from	כִּי אֶת־שֶׁבַע כְּבָשֹׂת
my hand,	תִּקַּח מִיָּדִי
so that you may be a witness for me	בַּעֲבוּר תִּהְיֶה־לִּי לְעֵדָה
that I dug this well [*be'er*]."	כִּי חָפַרְתִּי אֶת־הַבְּאֵר הַזֹּאת."
On account of this, he named	עַל־כֵּן קָרָא לַמָּקוֹם
that place "Beer-Sheva,"	הַהוּא בְּאֵר שָׁבַע
for there the two of them swore an	כִּי שָׁם נִשְׁבְּעוּ שְׁנֵיהֶם.
oath [*sheva*].	

[Gen. 21:29–31]

This story is also full of puns. "*Beer-Sheva*" can mean either the
"Well of the Seven [Lambs]" or the "Well of the Oath." Both have a
place in this story.

24

The Akedah, the Binding of Isaac, is one of the most famous stories in the Bible. It tells about God's supreme test of Abraham's faith in him.

Although Abraham had already shown his faith in God by leaving his ancestors and homeland to travel to a land which he had never seen, God devised one more extreme test for him:

After these things,	וַיְהִי אַחַר הַדְּבָרִים הָאֵלֶּה
God tested Abraham.	וְהָאֱלֹהִים נִסָּה אֶת־אַבְרָהָם.
He said to him, "Abraham."	וַיֹּאמֶר אֵלָיו אַבְרָהָם
And he answered, "Here I am."	וַיֹּאמֶר הִנֵּנִי.
Then he said, "Take your son,	וַיֹּאמֶר קַח־נָא אֶת־בִּנְךָ
your only one, whom you love, namely	אֶת־יְחִידְךָ אֲשֶׁר אָהַבְתָּ
Isaac,	אֶת־יִצְחָק
and go to the land of Moriah;	וְלֶךְ־לְךָ אֶל־אֶרֶץ הַמֹּרִיָּה
and offer him there as a burnt offering	וְהַעֲלֵהוּ שָׁם לְעֹלָה
upon one of the hills	עַל אַחַד הֶהָרִים
which I will tell you."	אֲשֶׁר אֹמַר אֵלֶיךָ.

[Gen 22:1–2]

PRAYER VOCABULARY

seven	שֶׁבַע	he tested	נִסָּה
lambs	כְּבָשֹׂת	your son	בִּנְךָ
as a witness	לְעֵדָה	and go	וְלֶךְ־לְךָ
I dug	חָפַרְתִּי	and offer him	וְהַעֲלֵהוּ
the well	הַבְּאֵר	as a burnt offering	לְעֹלָה
they swore	נִשְׁבְּעוּ		

25

ABRAHAM TRAVELS TO MORIAH

So Abraham arose early in the morning

and saddled his donkey

and took his two servants with him,

as well as his son Isaac.

He split wood for the burnt offering

and got up to go to the place

which God had commanded

him [to go].

וַיַּשְׁכֵּם אַבְרָהָם בַּבֹּקֶר

וַיַּחֲבֹשׁ אֶת־חֲמֹרוֹ

וַיִּקַּח אֶת־שְׁנֵי נְעָרָיו אִתּוֹ

וְאֵת יִצְחָק בְּנוֹ

וַיְבַקַּע עֲצֵי עֹלָה.

וַיָּקָם וַיֵּלֶךְ אֶל־הַמָּקוֹם

אֲשֶׁר־אָמַר־לוֹ הָאֱלֹהִים.

[Gen 22:3–4]

THE CLIMB TO MORIAH

As if in a dream or a nightmare, in which one is driven to do something that would under normal circumstances be considered impossible, Abraham carried out God's command and set out to sacrifice his son. When they came close to Moriah, which is identified in Jewish tradition with the Temple Mount in Jerusalem, where the Moslem Dome of the Rock now stands, Abraham left his servants behind. Father and son continued by themselves. The Bible records a short but extremely expressive exchange that passed between them.

Isaac spoke to his father Abraham,

saying, "My father."

He answered, "Here I am, my son."

He asked, "Here are the fire and the wood,

but where is the lamb for the offering?"

Abraham answered,

"God will see to the lamb

for the offering, my son."

So the two of them went on their way together.

וַיֹּאמֶר יִצְחָק אֶל־אַבְרָהָם אָבִיו

וַיֹּאמֶר אָבִי

וַיֹּאמֶר הִנֶּנִּי בְנִי

וַיֹּאמֶר הִנֵּה הָאֵשׁ וְהָעֵצִים

וְאַיֵּה הַשֶּׂה לְעֹלָה?

וַיֹּאמֶר אַבְרָהָם

אֱלֹהִים יִרְאֶה־לּוֹ הַשֶּׂה

לְעֹלָה בְּנִי

וַיֵּלְכוּ שְׁנֵיהֶם יַחְדָּו.

[Gen 22:7–8]

Finally they got to their destination. Abraham built an altar, laid
out the wood, bound Isaac, and placed him on the wood in order to
sacrifice him. Just as he was lifting up the knife to slaughter his son:

*The Hebrew word here, וַיַּקֹד **("and he bound") gives us the name Akedah.**

THE ANGEL

A messenger of Adonai called to him from heaven,	וַיִּקְרָא אֵלָיו מַלְאַךְ יְהוָה מִן־הַשָּׁמַיִם
saying, "Abraham, Abraham!"	וַיֹּאמֶר "אַבְרָהָם אַבְרָהָם"
He answered, "Here I am."	וַיֹּאמֶר "הִנֵּנִי:"
He said, "Don't send forth your hand against the youth,	וַיֹּאמֶר "אַל־תִּשְׁלַח יָדְךָ אֶל־הַנַּעַר
and don't do anything to him!	וְאַל־תַּעַשׂ לוֹ מְאוּמָה
For now I know that you truly worship God,	כִּי יָדַעְתִּי כִּי־יְרֵא אֱלֹהִים אַתָּה
since you didn't even withhold	וְלֹא חָשַׂכְתָּ אֶת־בִּנְךָ
your only son from me."	אֶת־יְחִידְךָ מִמֶּנִּי."

[Gen 22:11–12]

PRAYER VOCABULARY

his donkey	חֲמֹרוֹ	two of them	שְׁנֵיהֶם
wood	עֲצֵי	together	יַחְדָּו
my father	אָבִי	a messenger	מַלְאַךְ
the fire	הָאֵשׁ	Here I am	הִנֵּנִי
and the wood	וְהָעֵצִים	the youth	הַנַּעַר
the lamb	הַשֶּׂה	anything	מְאוּמָה

27

THE RAM

When Abraham looked up, he saw a ram caught in the thicket, which he then sacrificed in place of Isaac. God had indeed provided the "lamb" for the offering!

On account of Abraham's trust in God, going so far as to be ready to sacrifice the son miraculously born to him and Sarah late in their lives, and the only tangible sign of the fulfillment of the covenant that God had made with him, God renewed his covenant with Abraham and his descendants through Isaac.

The last few verses of Genesis 22 inform us of the birth of Rebecca, Isaac's cousin and future wife.

THE AKEDAH AND ROSH HASHANAH

Why are these two chapters read on Rosh Hashanah? There are a few possible answers.

First, in the medieval period in Europe, a time of intense persecutions of Jews beginning with the First Crusade, the story of the Akedah served as an inspirational model for parents who would often have to kill their own children in an act of *Kiddush Hashem* (Sanctification of the Name) in order to save them from what they considered to be an even worse fate.

Second, some feel that the inclusion by the rabbis of the story of Isaac's miraculous birth and return from nearly being dead are reactions to Christian stories about the birth and resurrection of Jesus. The rabbis, drawing on a pre-Christian Jewish tradition found in the Book of Jubilees, connected the sacrifice of Isaac with the theme of forgiveness on Rosh Hashanah. The horns of the ram caught in the thicket would thus be symbolic of the shofar that is blown on Rosh Hashanah (which is made from a ram's horn). This interpretation would show that much of what Christians claim as being unique about Jesus had been accomplished by Isaac.

Definitely in the first, but also apparently in the second reason, one can see the remnant of a popular belief that Isaac was actually sacrificed by Abraham and was subsequently brought back to life by God.

Nowadays there is a third reason. The Hebrew word for "burnt offering" (עוֹלָה) can also be translated into English as *holocaust*. The English word comes from the Greek, where it means the same as the Hebrew. In the translation of the Bible into Greek, the Septuagint, the word "holocaust" is used for the first time in this story. Just as the future of the Jewish people was nearly extinguished by the death of Isaac, so too in our century was the existence of the Jewish people nearly extinguished by the Holocaust. Just as Isaac returned from the brink of death to be one of the main ancestors of the Jews, so too have the Jewish people returned from the brink of destruction to a new vitality. The Akedah is a story that has given and continues to give inspiration and hope to the oppressed over the course of the centuries.

יוֹם כִּפּוּר
YOM KIPPUR

Coming at the end of the Yamim Nora'im, Yom Kippur is the culmination of all these days of repentance. The special quality of the day is evident when first entering the synagogue. The sanctuary is filled to overflowing. People are wearing their best clothing. The mood is solemn. Even the service is different. The opening "prayer" of the Yom Kippur service is the *Kol Nidre* ("all vows"), in which we state that we are released from all the vows which we made in the past year:

Our vows are not vows.	נִדְרָנָא לָא נִדְרֵי.
Our bonds are not bonds.	וֶאֱסָרָנָא לָא אֱסָרֵי.
Our oaths are not oaths.	וּשְׁבוּעָתָנָא לָא שְׁבוּעוֹת.

Like the Shabbat service, the Yom Kippur service contains the Shema Israel and the Amidah (silent prayer). There is also a Torah reading in the morning. However, what makes the Yom Kippur service different is the repeated confession of wrongdoing and the asking for forgiveness.

CONFESSION

The act of confession, called וִדּוּי , is an extremely important part of the service. Without the admission of guilt, there can be no forgiveness. The Jewish community as a whole confesses to quite a number of sins, even though the individual members of the community most probably have not committed the majority of these acts. There are two lists of sins that are confessed in the Mahzor. The longer confession is known as the עַל חֵטְא ("for the sin") and lists a whole series of guilty acts which we may have committed:

For the sin we have committed before you by speaking slander.	וְעַל חֵטְא שֶׁחָטָאנוּ לְפָנֶיךָ בִּלְשׁוֹן הָרָע.
For the sin we have committed before you by cheating in business.	עַל חֵטְא שֶׁחָטָאנוּ לְפָנֶיךָ בְּמַשָׂא וּבְמַתָּן.

And for the sin we have committed
  before you
  by hurting other people.
	עַל חֵטְא שֶׁחָטָאנוּ
	לְפָנֶיךָ
	בְּהוֹנָאַת רֵעַ.

PRAYER VOCABULARY

our vows	נִדְרָנָא	for the sin	עַל חֵטְא
our bonds	וֶאֱסָרָנָא	we have committed	שֶׁחָטָאנוּ
our oaths	וּשְׁבוּעָתָנָא	by cheating in business	בְּמַשָׂא וּבְמַתָּן
		by hurting other people	בְּהוֹנָאַת רֵעַ

Focus on Kol Nidre

Kol Nidre is not really a prayer. It is a legal formula. We don't know when it was written or who wrote it, but we do know that it was used as far back as the eighth century C.E. (common era). Like other Jewish legal texts, the Kol Nidre is written in Aramaic, a language related to Hebrew and spoken by Jews for many centuries. The Kol Nidre is intended to free Jews from the obligations which they have made to God. During times of persecution, enemies of the Jews would point to the Kol Nidre as evidence that Jews couldn't be trusted, since they had a legal formula allowing them to go back on their word. In the Jewish understanding, Kol Nidre and the Yom Kippur services deal *only* with the relationship between God and humanity. In other words, if one person commits a wrong against another person, asking God's forgiveness on Yom Kippur doesn't help. You must ask the wronged person's forgiveness directly, during the Yamim Nora'im. In Jewish belief, you have to ask forgiveness of the one you hurt, be it God or another person. Yom Kippur is the day on which we ask God's forgiveness.

The shorter confession, known as the וְדּוּי , is a list of a series of possible sins. Each concept is represented by one word, and the words are listed in alphabetical order:

Aleph	We have sinned.	אָשַׁמְנוּ.
Bet	We have acted treacherously.	בָּגַדְנוּ.
Gimel	We have stolen.	גָּזַלְנוּ.
Dalet	We have slandered.	דִּבַּרְנוּ דֹפִי.

Focus on the Vidui

The Vidui is not the only Hebrew prayer that is written in alphabetical order. This style was quite common, especially in poetry. In the Bible, parts of the Book of Eicha, or Lamentations, were written alphabetically. Many psalms were also written in this style. Why was this done? Some people believe that this type of writing was meant to express the thoughts on a subject "from A to Z." Others say that it was an artistic challenge. During the Middle Ages, when poetry was written specifically for the Siddur, acrostic, or alphabetic, writing was also widely employed, but with a twist. Sometimes the poet would go through the Hebrew alphabet *backwards!* At other times, the writer would write a poem in such a way that if you put the first letters of each line together, they would spell the author's name. These poems were meant to help people pray, but the alphabetic games were used to memorialize the author and to make sure people didn't get bored during services.

Every time in the service that such a confession is recited, it is followed by a reminder of Israel's relation with God. This is recited in the hope that the remembrance of this special relationship will help avert a harsh judgment.

For we are your people,	כִּי אָנוּ עַמֶּךָ
and you are our God.	וְאַתָּה אֱלֹהֵינוּ.
We are your flock,	אָנוּ צֹאנֶךָ
and you are our Shepherd.	וְאַתָּה רוֹעֵנוּ.
We are your vineyard,	אָנוּ כַרְמֶךָ
and you are our Keeper.	וְאַתָּה נוֹטְרֵנוּ.

We next ask God to forgive us for the sins which we have just finished reciting. In Jewish belief, it is not enough just to recite the offenses, a person must really be sorry for these wrongs, even if that person didn't actually commit all the sins recited. Not only that, you must really want to change your behavior when asking for forgiveness, otherwise the confession isn't considered sincere.

This act of confessing wrong and asking forgiveness is repeated at all the Yom Kippur services. This includes the evening (Kol Nidre) service, the morning service, and the additional service (Musaf). The mood of confession and repentance reaches a climax at the very last service on Yom Kippur, the נְעִילָה ("closing") service.

PRAYER VOCABULARY

your people	עַמֶּךָ
your flock	צֹאנֶךָ
our Shepherd	רוֹעֵנוּ
our Keeper	נוֹטְרֵנוּ

Focus on Two Special Yom Kippur Services

Like Shabbat and other holy days, Yom Kippur begins with the evening service. This is followed by the morning service, Musaf (additional) service, and the afternoon service. There is also a service called יִזְכּוֹר ("remembrance"). This is a special memorial service which is held on certain Jewish holidays. Every person who has lost a family member takes part in this service to remember and honor the dead. There is also a service which is unique to Yom Kippur. It is called the עֲבוֹדָה ("service"). Avodah refers to a ceremony that took place when the Temple existed in Jerusalem. On Yom Kippur the high priest would enter the Holy of Holies of the Temple. This was the only time that anyone was allowed to go into that most holy place. Since there is no more Temple in Jerusalem, and consequently no high priest, the Avodah service takes the place of that ceremony. The modern Avodah service consists of describing what the high priest would do at that time. Many rabbis, and even occasionally some worshippers, act out the motions that the high priest would go through at this ancient Temple service and bow down before the ark in the synagogue. This is the only time that a Jew ever bows down in worship.

"THE CLOSING OF THE GATES"

Neilah is the very last service of Yom Kippur. The word Neilah means "closing." It is taken to symbolize the gates of heaven closing at the end of Yom Kippur. What makes Neilah different from the other Yom Kippur services is our awareness that time is running out. Try to imagine running to get through a door before it closes. You put all your strength into the effort. That's the type of feeling that exists at Neilah. Special prayers are recited at Neilah that help to intensify this mood:

Open the gate for us,	פְּתַח לָנוּ שַׁעַר,
now that the gate is closing,	בְּעֵת נְעִילַת שַׁעַר
for the day is fading.	כִּי פָנָה יוֹם.
The day is fading,	הַיּוֹם יִפְנֶה,
the sun is setting,	הַשֶּׁמֶשׁ יָבֹא וְיִפְנֶה
let us through your gates.	נָבוֹאָה שְׁעָרֶיךָ.

FORGIVENESS

This is our last chance to ask forgiveness, and so we put all our remaining strength into praying for repentance. During Neilah we repeat with special feeling the confessions that we have made during all of Yom Kippur. We repeat our praises of God and acknowledge his power. Finally, the sun is setting, the day is ending, we have done our best to ask for a merciful judgment. We hope that the response will be one of forgiveness:

And Adonai said,	וַיֹּאמֶר יְהֹוָה
"I have forgiven according to your word."	"סָלַחְתִּי כִּדְבָרֶךָ".

Each one of us has done everything possible to ask for a merciful judgment for the whole community. No matter what the final decree, the very last thing we do is reaffirm our faith in God. We do this by repeating a number of familiar lines:

Hear, O Israel,   שְׁמַע יִשְׂרָאֵל,

   Adonai is our God, Adonai is one.   יְיָ אֱלֹהֵינוּ יְיָ אֶחָד!

[Said once]

Blessed is his glorious kingdom   בָּרוּךְ שֵׁם כְּבוֹד מַלְכוּתוֹ

   forever and ever. *[Repeated 3 times.]*   לְעוֹלָם וָעֶד.

Adonai is God. *[Repeated 7 times.]*   יְהֹוָה הוּא הָאֱלֹהִים.

By now it is dark outside. Our prayers are finished. The shofar is sounded, and Yom Kippur is officially over.

PRAYER VOCABULARY

gate	שַׁעַר
closing	נְעִילַת
the sun	הַשֶּׁמֶשׁ
your gates	שְׁעָרֶיךָ
according to your word	כִּדְבָרֶךְ
his kingdom	מַלְכוּתוֹ

יוֹנָה
THE BOOK OF JONAH

THE FIRST CALL

As the culmination of the Yamim Nora'im, the Days of Awe, Yom Kippur stands as *the* day of repentance in Jewish life. It is the day on which the Jewish community as a whole stands before God and asks for forgiveness of its shortcomings. It is only appropriate that the special reading at the afternoon service on Yom Kippur should deal with the theme of repentance. This is indeed one of the major themes of the Book of Jonah.

Although Jonah is not one of the Five Megillot, it is often grouped with them, since it is one of the short books of the Bible read in its entirety on a Jewish holiday. The Book of Jonah is actually the fifth of the twelve books of the minor prophets, which together count as the eighth and last book of the Nevi'im (Prophets). Unlike the rest of the "Twelve," the Book of Jonah is not a collection of the famous prophecies of a particular prophet. Jonah tells a story, a story about a reluctant prophet, his successful mission, and what God teaches him about repentance and his own importance.

The Book of Jonah starts in a direct manner:

The word of Adonai came to Jonah,	וַיְהִי דְּבַר־יְהֹוָה אֶל־יוֹנָה,
the son of Amittai, saying:	בֶּן־אֲמִתַּי, לֵאמֹר:
"Get up! Go to Nineveh, the great city,	"קוּם! לֵךְ אֶל־נִינְוֵה, הָעִיר הַגְּדוֹלָה
and cry out against it.	וּקְרָא עָלֶיהָ.
For their evil has come to my attention."	כִּי־עָלְתָה רָעָתָם לְפָנָי.

[Jon 1:1–2]

PRAYER VOCABULARY

get up	קוּם	
the city	הָעִיר	
their evil	רָעָתָם	

Focus on Jonah and His Mission

Jonah is one of the few prophets who is mentioned in one of the historical books of the Bible. In a summary of the reign of Jeroboam II, who ruled the northern kingdom of Israel from 786 to 746 B.C.E., the Second Book of Kings 14:25 recounts how Jeroboam extended the borders of Israel to the north, "according to the word of Adonai, the God of Israel, which he spoke through his servant, Jonah the son of Amittai, the prophet from Gat-Hepher." The city to which he was sent, Nineveh, was one of the great cities of the ancient world. It reached its greatest fame and power as the capital of the mighty Assyrian empire, which conquered most of the ancient Near East; yet it was itself conquered by the Medes and the Babylonians in 612 B.C.E. The largest collection of the ancient literature of Mesopotamia was found in the ruins of Nineveh, in the library of King Ashurbanipal. On account of its deserved reputation as a cruel military state, Assyria and its capital, Nineveh, became symbols of cruelty and wickedness. No wonder God sent a prophet to prophesy against Nineveh! But what was his purpose in sending a prophet there?

Many of the great prophets and leaders of the Jews in the Bible were reluctant to accept their missions from God: Moses because he stuttered, Jeremiah because he was too young. However, both Moses and Jeremiah spoke with God and worked out their problems. Not so Jonah!

So Jonah got up to flee to Tarshish	וַיָּקָם יוֹנָה לִבְרֹחַ תַּרְשִׁישָׁה
from before Adonai.	מִלִּפְנֵי יְהֹוָה.
He went down to Yafo and found a ship	וַיֵּרֶד יָפוֹ וַיִּמְצָא אֳנִיָּה
on its way to Tarshish.	בָּאָה תַרְשִׁישׁ.
He paid its fare	וַיִּתֵּן שְׂכָרָהּ
and boarded it in order to go	וַיֵּרֶד בָּהּ לָבוֹא
with them to Tarshish	עִמָּהֶם תַּרְשִׁישָׁה
from before Adonai.	מִלִּפְנֵי יְהֹוָה.

[Jon 1:3]

This verse emphasizes geography. Jonah was in the land of Israel, whose major port city was Yafo (Jaffa), just to the south of modern Tel-Aviv. God sent Jonah to Nineveh, which lay in Mesopotamia, far to the east. So what did Jonah do? He went and found the first ship going to Tarshish, which was probably in Spain, the westernmost point of the known world!

PRAYER VOCABULARY

to flee	לִבְרֹחַ
a ship	אֳנִיָּה
its fare	שְׂכָרָהּ

THE STORM

Once Jonah was on the ship, God caused an enormous storm to rage. While the rest of the sailors were crying to their gods for help and throwing unnecessary objects overboard in order to keep the ship from sinking, Jonah lay down and went to sleep. Finally the sailors cast lots in order to find out on whose account the storm was raging. Jonah was the one chosen. When the sailors asked him what he was doing and where he was from, Jonah answered:

I am a Hebrew	עִבְרִי אָנֹכִי.
I worship Adonai, God of Heaven,	וְאֶת־יְהֹוָה אֱלֹהֵי הַשָּׁמַיִם אֲנִי יָרֵא,
who created the sea and dry land.	אֲשֶׁר־עָשָׂה אֶת־הַיָּם וְאֶת־הַיַּבָּשָׁה.

[Jon 1:9]

PRAYER VOCABULARY

the sea	אֶת־הַיָּם	
(and) the dry land	וְאֶת־הַיַּבָּשָׁה	

The sailors were afraid of God and asked Jonah what to do to quiet his anger. Jonah told them to throw him overboard. But the sailors didn't want to murder an innocent person. So they tried harder than ever to row back to shore. When they saw that they were getting nowhere, and the storm was getting worse, they threw Jonah overboard with a prayer to God not to hold them guilty for the spilling of innocent blood. Immediately the storm stopped and the ship was saved. Thereupon the sailors worshipped God and offered him sacrifices.

THE FISH

But Jonah did not die:

God appointed a large fish to swallow Jonah. וַיְמַן יְהֹוָה דָּג גָּדוֹל לִבְלֹעַ אֶת־יוֹנָה.

And Jonah was in the belly of the fish וַיְהִי יוֹנָה בִּמְעֵי הַדָּג

for three days and three nights שְׁלֹשָׁה יָמִים וּשְׁלֹשָׁה לֵילוֹת.

[Jon 2:1]

PRAYER VOCABULARY	
a fish	דָּג
to swallow	לִבְלֹעַ
in the belly	בִּמְעֵי

Focus on the Fish

Although the fish has traditionally been called a whale, the Bible just states that it was a large fish. This is similar to the generic fruit that Adam and Eve ate in the Garden of Eden, which is popularly called an apple. Later generations always try to make specific that which the Bible leaves vague. As we try to rationalize the swallowing of Jonah by ascribing it to the largest fish that we know, the whale, we detract from the story. The story is relating an essentially miraculous event, one which cannot be described by rational means.

What follows is a psalm, a poem, in the form of a song of thanksgiving after deliverance from a great distress. Because it doesn't refer directly to Jonah's situation, many modern scholars have considered it a later addition to the book. However, an examination of the structure of the book reveals that it has to have been an integral part of the book from its beginning, whether it was actually written by the author of Jonah or quoted by him from another source. The first and third chapters of the book focus on the non-Jews and their religiosity. The second and fourth chapters focus on Jonah's reactions to his situation. Without this beautiful psalm, chapter 2 would be very short indeed.

JONAH'S PLIGHT

I called to Adonai in my distress,	קָרָאתִי מִצָּרָה לִי אֶל־יְהוָה,
and he answered me.	וַיַּעֲנֵנִי.
From the belly of Sheol [the underworld]	מִבֶּטֶן שְׁאוֹל
I cried for help.	שִׁוַּעְתִּי.
You have heard my voice.	שָׁמַעְתָּ קוֹלִי.

[Jon 2:3]

The waters encircled me,	אֲפָפוּנִי מַיִם עַד־נֶפֶשׁ,
the deep surrounded me,	תְּהוֹם יְסֹבְבֵנִי,
weeds were twisted about my head.	סוּף חָבוּשׁ לְרֹאשִׁי.

[Jon 2:6]

HE REMEMBERS GOD

When my soul grew faint in me,	בְּהִתְעַטֵּף עָלַי נַפְשִׁי,
I remembered Adonai.	אֶת־יְהוָה זָכָרְתִּי.
My prayer came to you,	וַתָּבוֹא אֵלֶיךָ תְּפִלָּתִי,
to your holy temple.	אֶל־הֵיכַל קָדְשֶׁךָ.

[Jon 2:8]

HE THANKS GOD

As for me, with a voice of thanksgiving
  I will offer you sacrifice.

That which I have vowed, I will fulfill.

Salvation belongs to Adonai.

וַאֲנִי בְּקוֹל תּוֹדָה
אֶזְבְּחָה־לָּךְ.
אֲשֶׁר נָדַרְתִּי אֲשַׁלֵּמָה.
יְשׁוּעָתָה לַיהֹוָה.

[Jon 2:10]

JONAH GETS TO LAND

Without further ado, the Bible relates that:

Adonai then commanded the fish,

  and it spit Jonah out on the dry land.

וַיֹּאמֶר יְהֹוָה לַדָּג
וַיָּקֵא אֶת־יוֹנָה אֶל־הַיַּבָּשָׁה.

[Jon 2:11]

THE SECOND CALL

Once again God called to Jonah to go to Nineveh and to prophesy against it:

The word of Adonai came to Jonah
  a second time.

"Get up! Go to Nineveh, the great city..

Call out to it that
  which I say to you."

וַיְהִי דְבַר־יְהֹוָה אֶל־יוֹנָה
שֵׁנִית לֵאמֹר.
"קוּם לֵךְ אֶל־נִינְוֵה הָעִיר הַגְּדוֹלָה
וּקְרָא אֵלֶיהָ אֶת־הַקְּרִיאָה
אֲשֶׁר אָנֹכִי דֹּבֵר אֵלֶיךָ."

[Jon 3:1–2]

PRAYER VOCABULARY			
in my distress	מִצָּרָה לִי	I remembered	זָכַרְתִּי
I cried for help	שִׁוַּעְתִּי	my prayer	תְּפִלָּתִי
waters	מַיִם	I have vowed	נָדַרְתִּי
the deep	תְּהוֹם	the dry land	הַיַּבָּשָׁה
about my head	לְרֹאשִׁי	the great city	הָעִיר הַגְּדוֹלָה

Having already found out that flight was useless, that God was truly God of the whole world, Jonah finally gave in and went to prophesy against Nineveh:

"Another forty days,

and Nineveh will be turned."

[Jon 3:4b]

עוֹד אַרְבָּעִים יוֹם

וְנִינְוֵה נֶהְפָּכֶת.

The word translated here as "turned" can mean either "destroyed" or "turned into something else/changed." Jonah, as we shall see, understood his prophecy to mean that in forty days Nineveh would be destroyed, just as God "destroyed" Sodom and Gomorrah in Genesis chapter 19, where the same word is used. However, the rabbis tell us that God used the term with an additional meaning in this story; since, to Jonah's surprise, the whole city of Nineveh, from the king to the children, and even the animals, believed in God and changed their ways. They fasted and put on sackcloth and ashes. These are the traditional signs of mourning and repentance. In Hebrew, the word for "repentance" also means "turning."

NINEVEH'S REPENTANCE AND GOD'S FORGIVENESS

God saw their actions,

that they had turned

from their evil ways.

So God repented of the evil

which he had said he would do to them

And he didn't do it.

וַיַּרְא הָאֱלֹהִים אֶת־מַעֲשֵׂיהֶם,

כִּי־שָׁבוּ

מִדַּרְכָּם הָרָעָה.

וַיִּנָּחֶם הָאֱלֹהִים עַל־הָרָעָה

אֲשֶׁר־דִּבֶּר לַעֲשׂוֹת־לָהֶם

וְלֹא־עָשָׂה.

[Jon 3:10]

PRAYER VOCABULARY

40 days	אַרְבָּעִים יוֹם	
their actions	מַעֲשֵׂיהֶם	
the evil	הָרָעָה	

When God decided not to destroy Nineveh, Jonah got furious. Unlike Abraham, who tried to bargain with God in order to cancel his decision to destroy Sodom and Gomorrah, Jonah was angry that God had mercy on Nineveh.

JONAH'S ANGER

Jonah was so angry about the mercy granted to Nineveh that he asked God to take his life. Jonah claimed that he had known from the beginning that God was merciful. That was the reason why he hadn't wanted to go to Nineveh in the first place. (Because it was a waste of time? Because he didn't want to be a false prophet?) Now he went out from the city into the desert. There God caused a plant to grow to provide Jonah with shade from the sun. This plant revived Jonah's spirit, and he finally was happy about something. However, at dawn the next morning, God caused a worm to infect the plant and make it wither. The sun beat down on Jonah, and a hot wind blew past him. As he was fainting from the heat, Jonah once again asked God to take his life. When God asked Jonah if it was worth being so upset about the loss of the plant, Jonah answered that it was.

GOD'S ANSWER

And God said:

"You pity the plant,

on which you expended no effort,

and which you did not raise;

which grew in one night,

and perished in one night.

וַיֹּאמֶר יְהוָֹה:

"אַתָּה חַסְתָּ עַל־הַקִּיקָיוֹן,

אֲשֶׁר לֹא־עָמַלְתָּ בּוֹ

וְלֹא גִדַּלְתּוֹ

שֶׁבִּן־לַיְלָה הָיָה

וּבִן־לַיְלָה אָבָד.

45

But I should not pity Nineveh,

   the great city,

      in which there are more than

         120,000 people

           who do not know their right

             from their left,

                and many animals?"

וַאֲנִי לֹא אָחוּס עַל־נִינְוֵה

הָעִיר הַגְּדוֹלָה

אֲשֶׁר יֶשׁ־בָּהּ הַרְבֵּה

מִשְׁתֵּים־עֶשְׂרֵה רִבּוֹ אָדָם

אֲשֶׁר לֹא־יָדַע בֵּין־יְמִינוֹ

לִשְׂמֹאלוֹ,

וּבְהֵמָה רַבָּה. "

[Jon 4:10–11]

PRAYER VOCABULARY	
the plant	הַקִּיקָיוֹן
night	לַיְלָה
their right	יְמִינוֹ
from their left	לִשְׂמֹאלוֹ

    With this question the Book of Jonah comes to an end. The point is made. God is a merciful God, who cares for all of his creation. Unlike Jonah, who seemed to care more about his own reputation, God wants people to repent of their ways. It is only at the end of the book that God finally revealed to Jonah the real reason for his going to Nineveh. It was not to destroy, but to save. If Jonah could show pity for a simple plant with which he had nothing to do, should God not show mercy for the people and animals of his creation?

46

On Yom Kippur we all stand before God and ask his forgiveness for our sins. Only God has the power to forgive. He alone knows who is sincere and who isn't. Yet this solemn day is actually a day of rejoicing. For God delights in the return of those who are evil from their wicked path. As such, Yom Kippur is a day of renewal. After Yom Kippur we can all start with a renewed relationship with God and the world. This is what the reading of Jonah on Yom Kippur wishes to emphasize.

Focus on Why Jonah Was Angry

Traditional commentators such as Rashi (Rabbi Solomon ben Isaac, who lived in northern France from 1040 to 1105 C.E.) and Radak (Rabbi David Kimhi, who lived from about 1160 to about 1235 in southern France) find two reasons for Jonah's anger. First, Jonah felt that since his prophecy did not come true, the Ninevites would feel that he was a false prophet, which would cause them to scorn the God who had sent him. Second, Jonah felt that by causing the Ninevites to repent, he was placing the Israelites in a bad light, since they themselves would not repent. However, it is difficult to understand the end of the book if one adopts such a positive attitude toward Jonah. It is possible that God chose a reluctant person such as Jonah in order to teach him a lesson about divine mercy and his own self-importance. As indicated above, the possibility exists that Jonah misunderstood the message that he was to deliver to the Ninevites. Jonah thought that he was supposed to preach the doom of Nineveh. God seems to have wanted Jonah to preach salvation and repentance.

הַסֻּכָּה
THE SUKKAH: AN "OPEN HOUSE"

In ancient Israel, the sukkah was a temporary shelter used by farmers gathering the fall harvest. Even when Jews no longer farmed, the holiday of Sukkot kept the symbol of the sukkah, but the meaning of this symbol changed. In time, the sukkah not only served as a reminder of ancient Israelite farmers and the fall harvest, but it also came to symbolize the temporary shelters that the Israelites lived in during their years of wandering in the Sinai desert after the Exodus from Egypt. Thus, the sukkah is used to recall our Jewish heritage.

It is customary to dwell in the sukkah. This means eating in the sukkah, or even sleeping in it. The sukkah becomes a temporary home. Like a regular home, guests are invited, especially on holidays. One tradition that makes Sukkot special is inviting famous people from Jewish history to be guests in the sukkah. There is a special prayer for this called *Ushpizin*. Ushpizin is the Aramaic word for "guests." Ushpizin is an invitation, in Aramaic, to a number of biblical figures.

Focus on Aramaic

It is a common belief that Jewish prayers are all in Hebrew. While it is true that most of Jewish liturgy is in Hebrew, some is in Aramaic. Aramaic is a language related to Hebrew. It became the daily language of the Jews during the Babylonian exile and continued in this function when the Jews returned to Israel. Among Jewish prayers in Aramaic are the *Kol Nidrei, Ushpizin,* and *Ha-Lachma Anya* ("the bread of poverty"), which is in the Passover Haggadah. The Talmud is written in Aramaic, as is the marriage contract, the *Ketubah.*

I invite to my meal these heavenly guests: אֲזַמִּין לִסְעֻדָתִי, אוּשְׁפִּיזִין עִלָּאִין:

Abraham and Sarah,	אַבְרָהָם וְשָׂרָה,
Isaac and Rebecca,	יִצְחָק וְרִבְקָה,
Jacob, Leah, and Rachel,	יַעֲקֹב רָחֵל וְלֵאָה,
Joseph,	יוֹסֵף,
Moses, Aaron, and Miriam,	מֹשֶׁה, אַהֲרֹן, מִרְיָם,
and David.	וְדָוִד.

Each day, the invitation is addressed to a different group in the list. Those people are asked if it is all right for all the other biblical figures mentioned to join in the meal.

First day

May it please you, Abraham and Sarah,

  my heavenly guests,

that all the other heavenly guests

dwell here with me and you.

בְּמָטוּ מִנְּכוֹן אַבְרָהָם וְשָׂרָה
אוּשְׁפִּיזִי עִלָּאִי,
דְּיַתְבֵי עִמִּי וְעִמָּךְ
כָּל אוּשְׁפִּיזֵי עִלָּאִי.

Second day

May it please you, Isaac and Rebecca,

  my heavenly guests,

that all the heavenly guests

dwell here with me and with you.

בְּמָטוּ מִנְּכוֹן יִצְחָק וְרִבְקָה,
אוּשְׁפִּיזִי עִלָּאִי,
דְּיַתְבֵי עִמִּי וְעִמָּךְ
כָּל אוּשְׁפִּיזֵי עִלָּאִי.

This ceremony of invitation goes on for seven days.

Ushpizin originated with the mystics of Safed. They believed that Jews who dwelled in the sukkah were entitled to have God's presence there. In addition to God, they believed that a number of God's faithful helpers, including some of the biblical figures mentioned in Ushpizin, also entered the sukkah. These biblical figures would see how their descendants celebrated Sukkot, as good Jews protected by God.

Sukkah	סֻכָּה (סֻכּוֹת)	the heavenly guests	אוּשְׁפִּיזִי עִלָּאֵי
I invite	אֲזַמִּין	with me	עִמִּי
to my meal	לִסְעֻדָּתִי	and you	וְעִמָּךְ

Focus on Mystical Beliefs

In the fifteenth and sixteenth centuries, the mystics of Safed, which lies in the Galilean hills in northern Israel, believed that the world and heaven consisted of a number of spheres. Humanity was created in one of the higher spheres. God rested in the highest sphere of all. Mysticism was seen as a way of bringing God's presence, the *Shechinah,* within people's reach in the lowest sphere of heaven. The mystics, led by Rabbi Joseph Caro, sought many ways to make it possible for people to reach the *Shechinah.* The main focus lay in trying to achieve spiritual purity. People found much of the mystics' work to be very moving. This is true to such an extent that many non-mystics borrowed mystical traditions. For example, *Kabbalat Shabbat,* the Friday evening service that welcomes the Shabbat, is a mystical creation still popular today. The purpose of this service can be found in the song that begins the service, *Lecha Dodi.* The Sabbath is welcomed as a bride. This is meant to spiritually unite the Jews with God's presence in order to enhance the celebration of Shabbat. Shabbat thus becomes more than a day of rest, it is a time of spiritual enjoyment.

קֹהֶלֶת

KOHELET: THE UNCHANGING CYCLE OF LIFE

After the Exodus from Egypt and the giving of the Torah, the holiday of Sukkot gained new meaning, based on biblical history. The sukkah, the temporary shelter which served to protect the farmers from the heat of the noonday sun, now became a symbol of the makeshift huts that the Israelites had erected and lived in during their forty years of wandering in the desert after leaving Egypt.

At Sukkot time one is very aware of the cycle of the seasons. The days are getting short, and winter is just around the corner. It is a time of year when one pauses and reflects on the passing of life and nature. Therefore, it is appropriate that the special reading for the Shabbat of Sukkot (or for Shemini Atzeret if there is no intermediate Shabbat during Sukkot) is the world-weary *Book of Kohelet*.

The Book of Kohelet, also known as *Ecclesiastes* or *The Preacher* in in English Bibles, is written from the perspective of someone who is approaching the end of his life. In his reflecting back on his life and what he learned from it, Kohelet left us with the book that bears his name. The Book of Kohelet is a collection of Kohelet's thoughts about the way of the world and the purpose of life. It can only have been written by someone who had lived a long life, and who had spent a good deal of time thinking about what he had experienced. For that reason, it was chosen to be read in the synagogue at the passing of nature's year.

As an old man, Kohelet looks back on his own life and muses about the purpose and aim of human life in general:

"Vanity of vanities" says Kohelet,

"הֲבֵל־הֲבָלִים" אָמַר קֹהֶלֶת

"Vanity of vanities, everything is vanity!" ".הֲבֵל הֲבָלִים הַכֹּל הָבֶל"

[Koh 1:2]

PRAYER VOCABULARY

vanity of vanities	הֲבֵל הַבְלִים
everything is vanity	הַכֹּל הָבֶל

Focus on Kohelet—the Person

The Book of Kohelet tells us very little personal information about Kohelet. However, Jewish tradition has an answer to the question of Kohelet's identity. The heading of the book calls Kohelet "the son of David, king in Jerusalem." He also refers to himself at one point as the "king over Israel in Jerusalem" Since only one son of David became king, and since that son was also known for his wisdom, Jewish tradition identifies Kohelet with King Solomon. This traditional view is supported by the tradition that two other books of the Bible, Proverbs and the Song of Songs, were also written by Solomon. According to the Midrash, Solomon wrote the Song of Songs with its emphasis on love when he was young, Proverbs with its practical wisdom when he was a mature adult, and Kohelet with its experienced hindsight when he was an old man. On the other hand, the consensus of modern biblical scholarship is that Kohelet was a teacher of "wisdom" in Jerusalem during the third century B.C.E. That conclusion is based on an analysis of the language, style, and thought of Kohelet, all of which seems to place him in the early Hellenistic period of Jewish history.

This outburst, which runs like a theme through the book, expresses Kohelet's view of life in a nutshell. What is the use of anything? Everything that a human being does in life to acquire riches or fame is vain and purposeless:

What does a person gain from all of his work

which he does under the sun?

מַה־יִּתְרוֹן לָאָדָם בְּכָל־עֲמָלוֹ

שֶׁיַּעֲמֹל תַּחַת הַשָּׁמֶשׁ?

One generation comes, another generation goes,

but the earth exists forever.

דּוֹר הֹלֵךְ וְדוֹר בָּא

וְהָאָרֶץ לְעוֹלָם עֹמֶדֶת.

[Koh 1:3–4]

What was is what will be.

What was done is what will be done.

There is absolutely nothing new under the sun!

מַה־שֶּׁהָיָה הוּא שֶׁיִּהְיֶה

וּמַה־שֶּׁנַּעֲשָׂה הוּא שֶׁיֵּעָשֶׂה.

וְאֵין כָּל־חָדָשׁ תַּחַת הַשָּׁמֶשׁ.

[Koh 1:9]

PRAYER VOCABULARY

generation	דּוֹר	what was	מַה־שֶּׁהָיָה
forever	לְעוֹלָם	is what will be	הוּא שֶׁיִּהְיֶה

THE END OF LIFE

Kohelet then considers the sense of slaving away all of one's life in order to acquire possessions or wisdom. What advantage does one have from all of one's toil? Whether you are rich or poor, wise or foolish, the end is the same. What is the sense then of denying oneself in order to gain something which one will not have the time to enjoy, or which will be wasted by whoever comes after you? Thus Kohelet comes to his major conclusion concerning the purpose of life:

There is nothing better for a person

than that he should eat and drink

and be pleased with his work.

This I also saw

is from the hand of God.

אֵין־טוֹב בָּאָדָם

שֶׁיֹּאכַל וְשָׁתָה

וְהֶרְאָה אֶת־נַפְשׁוֹ טוֹב בַּעֲמָלוֹ.

גַּם־זֶה רָאִיתִי אָנִי

כִּי מִיַּד הָאֱלֹהִים הִיא.

[Koh 2:24]

Life should be experienced and enjoyed in all of its variety, since it is a gift from God. It is a precious gift which should not be abused or misused, but should be taken advantage of for better or worse.

For everything there is a season,

    and a time for each matter under heaven:

A time to be born,

    and a time to die;

a time to plant,

    and a time to uproot that which is

        planted;

a time to kill,

    and a time to heal;

a time to tear down,

    and a time to build;

a time to cry,

    and a time to laugh;

a time to mourn,

    and a time to dance;

a time to throw stones,

    and a time to gather stones;

a time to hug,

    and a time to refrain from hugging;

a time to seek,

    and a time to lose;

a time to save,

    and a time to throw away;

לַכֹּל זְמָן

וְעֵת לְכָל־חֵפֶץ תַּחַת הַשָּׁמָיִם:

עֵת לָלֶדֶת,

וְעֵת לָמוּת;

עֵת לָטַעַת,

וְעֵת לַעֲקוֹר

נָטוּעַ;

עֵת לַהֲרוֹג,

וְעֵת לִרְפּוֹא;

עֵת לִפְרוֹץ

וְעֵת לִבְנוֹת;

עֵת לִבְכּוֹת,

וְעֵת לִשְׂחוֹק;

עֵת סְפוֹד,

וְעֵת רְקוֹד;

עֵת לְהַשְׁלִיךְ אֲבָנִים,

וְעֵת כְּנוֹס אֲבָנִים;

עֵת לַחֲבוֹק,

וְעֵת לִרְחֹק מֵחַבֵּק;

עֵת לְבַקֵּשׁ,

וְעֵת לְאַבֵּד;

עֵת לִשְׁמוֹר,

וְעֵת לְהַשְׁלִיךְ;

a time to tear apart,	עֵת לִקְרוֹעַ,
and a time to sew;	וְעֵת לִתְפּוֹר;
a time to be silent,	עֵת לַחֲשׁוֹת,
and a time to speak;	וְעֵת לְדַבֵּר;
a time to love,	עֵת לֶאֱהֹב,
and a time to hate;	וְעֵת לִשְׂנֹא;
a time for war	עֵת מִלְחָמָה,
and a time for peace.	וְעֵת שָׁלוֹם.

[Koh 3:1–8]

Although Kohelet counsels us to take all of life's events in stride, he does tell about the injustices he sees in the world, evil people who live happy lives, and good people who lead miserable lives. However, for Kohelet there is no sense in worrying about this. There is nothing that humankind can do to alter the world. All is in God's hands.

One should attempt to strive after wisdom, to be happy in one's work, and to live a morally good life, being moderate in everything that one does. For that is the lot of humanity.

PRAYER VOCABULARY

season	זְמָן	to laugh	לִשְׂחוֹק
a time	וְעֵת	to dance	רְקוֹד
to uproot	לַעֲקוֹר	to speak	לְדַבֵּר
to heal	לִרְפּוֹא	to hate	לִשְׂנֹא
to build	לִבְנוֹת		

MAN AND MAN

One should also be kind and considerate of one's fellows, since:

A good name is better than good oil.　　טוֹב שֵׁם מִשֶּׁמֶן טוֹב.

[Koh 7:1a]

In this sometimes difficult world of ours, it is good to remember the message of Kohelet:

THE JOY OF LIFE

Go, eat your bread joyfully,	לֵךְ אֱכֹל בְּשִׂמְחָה לַחְמֶךְ
and drink your wine with a happy heart,	וּשֲׁתֵה בְלֶב־טוֹב יֵינֶךָ
for God has already approved your	כִּי כְבָר רָצָה הָאֱלֹהִים
deeds.	אֶת־מַעֲשֶׂיךָ.
May your clothes be white (= clean) at all	בְּכָל־עֵת יִהְיוּ בְגָדֶיךָ לְבָנִים
times,	
and may oil not be lacking on your head.	וְשֶׁמֶן עַל־רֹאשְׁךָ אַל־יֶחְסָר
Enjoy life with the woman you love,	רְאֵה חַיִּים עִם־אִשָּׁה אֲשֶׁר־אָהַבְתָּ
all the days of your vain life,	כָּל־יְמֵי חַיֵּי הֶבְלֶךָ
which he has given you under the sun.	אֲשֶׁר נָתַן־לְךָ תַּחַת הַשֶּׁמֶשׁ
For that is your portion in life,	כִּי הוּא חֶלְקְךָ בַּחַיִּים
and in your work which you do	וּבַעֲמָלְךָ אֲשֶׁר־אַתָּה עָמֵל
under the sun.	תַּחַת הַשָּׁמֶשׁ.

[Koh 9:7–9]

PRAYER VOCABULARY

than good oil	מִשֶּׁמֶן טוֹב	your clothes	בְגָדֶיךָ
your bread	לַחְמֶךְ	your portion	חֶלְקְךָ
your wine	יֵינֶךָ	and in your work	וּבַעֲמָלְךָ
your deeds	מַעֲשֶׂיךָ		

57

Focus on a Similar Message

This message which Kohelet left to his students has a parallel in another ancient Near Eastern text, the Epic of Gilgamesh. This story from ancient Mesopotamia tells the tale of Gilgamesh's journey to the ends of the earth in search of immortality. During the course of his unsuccessful quest, he meets the goddess Siduri, who advises him in words which are very close to those of Kohelet:

Gilgamesh, where are you wandering?
You will not find the eternal life which you seek.
When the gods created humankind,
they established death for humankind.
They kept eternal life for themselves.
As for you, Gilgamesh, may your belly be full!
May you rejoice day and night!
Celebrate a festival each day!
Day and night dance and play!
Let your clothing be clean!
Let your head be bathed, may you be cleansed in water!
Pay attention to the little one who holds your hand!
May your wife be happy with you!
For this is the lot of humankind.

קְרִיאַת הַתּוֹרָה לְסֻכּוֹת
SUKKOT:
THE TORAH READING

On Sukkot, the Torah reading is taken for the most part from the Book of Leviticus, the third book of the Torah. In this book are to be found the most explicit regulations concerning the practice of the Jewish religion in the days when the Temple still stood. Among other laws, those concerning the celebration of various holidays are highlighted.

...donai spoke to Moses, saying,	וַיְדַבֵּר יְהֹוָה אֶל־מֹשֶׁה לֵּאמֹר,
...peak thus to the Israelites:	"דַּבֵּר אֶל־בְּנֵי יִשְׂרָאֵל לֵאמֹר
On the fifteenth day of this seventh month	בַּחֲמִשָּׁה עָשָׂר יוֹם לַחֹדֶשׁ הַשְּׁבִיעִי
is the festival of Sukkot,	הַזֶּה חַג הַסֻּכּוֹת
seven days [dedicated] to Adonai.	שִׁבְעַת יָמִים לַיהֹוָה.
...he first day is a holy occasion,	בַּיּוֹם הָרִאשׁוֹן מִקְרָא־קֹדֶשׁ
you shall not do any manner of work.	כָּל־מְלֶאכֶת עֲבֹדָה לֹא תַעֲשׂוּ.
...or seven days	שִׁבְעַת יָמִים
you shall bring a burnt offering to	תַּקְרִיבוּ אִשֶּׁה
Adonai.	לַיהֹוָה.

59

The eighth day

בַּיּוֹם הַשְּׁמִינִי

will be a holy occasion for you

מִקְרָא־קֹדֶשׁ יִהְיֶה לָכֶם

to bring a burnt offering to Adonai.

וְהִקְרַבְתֶּם אִשֶּׁה לַיהוָה

It is a day of assembly,

עֲצֶרֶת הִוא

you shall not do any manner of work!"

כָּל־מְלֶאכֶת עֲבֹדָה לֹא תַעֲשׂוּ!"

[Lev 23:33-36]

The eighth day of Sukkot has a special name, *Shemini Atzeret*, the Eighth Day of Assembly. The name is made up of two of the words used to describe it in this passage. It is discussed later in the book.

The Bible then goes on to reemphasize the practice of Sukkot and provides some additional details about its customs and celebrations.

MORE ON SUKKOT

Thus on the fifteenth day

אַךְ בַּחֲמִשָּׁה עָשָׂר יוֹם

of the seventh month,

לַחֹדֶשׁ הַשְּׁבִיעִי

when you gather the produce of

בְּאָסְפְּכֶם אֶת־תְּבוּאַת

the earth,

הָאָרֶץ

you shall celebrate the festival of Adonai

תָּחֹגּוּ אֶת־חַג־יְהוָֹה

for seven days,

שִׁבְעַת יָמִים

on the first day a day of rest,

בַּיּוֹם הָרִאשׁוֹן שַׁבָּתוֹן

and on the eighth day a day of rest.

וּבַיּוֹם הַשְּׁמִינִי שַׁבָּתוֹן.

[Lev 23:39]

PRAYER VOCABULARY			
the festival of Sukkot	חַג הַסֻּכּוֹת	the produce of	תְּבוּאַת
holy occasion	מִקְרָא־קֹדֶשׁ	you shall celebrate	תָּחֹגּוּ
work	עֲבֹדָה	a day of rest	שַׁבָּתוֹן
a day of assembly	עֲצֶרֶת		

After describing the fruit and branches with which to celebrate the holiday before Adonai, Leviticus goes on to repeat:

You shall celebrate it as a festival	וְחַגֹּתֶם אֹתוֹ חַג
for Adonai,	לַיהוָֹה
seven days in the year;	שִׁבְעַת יָמִים בַּשָּׁנָה
it is an eternal decree throughout your	חֻקַּת עוֹלָם לְדֹרֹתֵיכֶם
generations—	
in the seventh month	בַּחֹדֶשׁ הַשְּׁבִיעִי
you shall celebrate it.	תָּחֹגּוּ אֹתוֹ.
You shall dwell in huts [sukkot]	בַּסֻּכֹּת תֵּשְׁבוּ
for seven days,	שִׁבְעַת יָמִים
every citizen of Israel	כָּל־הָאֶזְרָח בְּיִשְׂרָאֵל
shall dwell in huts.	יֵשְׁבוּ בַּסֻּכֹּת.
In order that your generations shall know	לְמַעַן יֵדְעוּ דֹרֹתֵיכֶם
that I caused the children of Israel to	כִּי בַסֻּכּוֹת הוֹשַׁבְתִּי
dwell in huts	אֶת־בְּנֵי יִשְׂרָאֵל
when I brought them forth	בְּהוֹצִיאִי אוֹתָם
from the land of Egypt.	מֵאֶרֶץ מִצְרָיִם
I am Adonai, your God!	אֲנִי יְהוָֹה אֱלֹהֵיכֶם.

[Lev 23:41–43]

The celebration of Sukkot is a sign of the special relationship between God and the Jews. It is an active acknowledgment of the vital role that God has played, and continues to play, in Jewish history.

an eternal decree	חֻקַּת עוֹלָם	citizen	אֶזְרָח
you shall dwell	תֵּשְׁבוּ	your generations	דֹרֹתֵיכֶם

Focus on Lulav and Etrog

Together with the sukkah, the most well-known Sukkot symbols are the lulav and etrog. The lulav and etrog derive from a commandment in the Torah to gather *arba'at haminim,* the four species, on Sukkot. Leviticus 23:40 describes what the four species are: the fruit of goodly trees, which is the etrog (citron), the branches of palm trees (lulav), the boughs of leafy trees (myrtle), and willows of the brook (hoshanot). Since there are four species, why are there only two names? That's because what we call the lulav is made up of three of the species. The center of the lulav is the palm branch. In a holder on either side of it are the myrtle and willow branches. The four species represent a number of things in Judaism. The symbols range from the four-letter name of God to parts of the body. The etrog is the heart and shows humanity's serving God with wisdom. The lulav is the spine, representing upright service. The myrtle is the eyes, symbolizing enlightenment in God's service. The willow represents the lips, which say prayers to God.

PRAYER VOCABULARY

palm branch	לוּלָב
citron	אֶתְרוֹג
willow	עֲרָבָה
myrtle	הֲדַס

הוֹשַׁעְנָא רַבָּה
HOSHANA RABBA

Since Sukkot lasts such a long time, eight days, it has important days at the end as well as the beginning of the holiday. The seventh day of Sukkot is called Hoshana Rabba, meaning "the great Hoshana." Hoshana means "save us" in Aramaic. This name is taken from prayers that are repeated during Hoshana Rabba.

In ancient times Hoshana Rabba was tied in with the agricultural life of the Israelites. The Hoshana prayers ask for a good harvest in the coming year. In later times, it was popularly believed that Hoshana Rabba is an addition to Yom Kippur, and that on Hoshana Rabba God's decrees for the next year are finalized. The Hoshana prayers begin by asking God to save us. In asking this, we remind God of the different roles he has in relation to us:

The Hoshana prayers are recited while marching around the synagogue seven times. When asking God to save us, we remind him of how he saved our ancestors in the past. In so doing, we hope that God will be as merciful with us as with our ancestors. Throughout the seven processions and the numerous prayers recited, two words appear over and over: "save us!"

Save us!	הוֹשַׁע נָא!
For your sake, our God, save us!	לְמַעַנְךָ אֱלֹהֵינוּ, הוֹשַׁע נָא!
For your sake, our Creator, save us!	לְמַעַנְךָ בּוֹרְאֵנוּ. הוֹשַׁע נָא!
For your sake, our Redeemer, save us!	לְמַעַנְךָ גּוֹאֲלֵנוּ, הוֹשַׁע נָא!
For your sake, you who seek us, save us!	לְמַעַנְךָ דּוֹרְשֵׁנוּ, הוֹשַׁע נָא!
	הוֹשַׁע נָא!

PRAYER VOCABULARY

for your sake	לְמַעַנְךָ	our Redeemer	גּוֹאֲלֵנוּ
our Creator	בּוֹרְאֵנוּ	you who seek us	דּוֹרְשֵׁנוּ

שְׁמִינִי עֲצֶרֶת
SHEMINI ATZERET

The last day of Sukkot is called *Shemini Atzeret* or the "Eighth Day of Solemn Assembly." What makes this day unique is also tied in with our ancient agricultural roots. Sukkot marks the time of the fall harvest. Once this is ended, thoughts must turn to the spring harvest. Water is necessary for plants to grow. In the Land of Israel, the winter brings rain. On Shemini Atzeret, our thoughts turn to the coming winter and the distant spring harvest. Our concern is made evident by a special Shemini Atzeret prayer, the *Tefillat Geshem*, the prayer for rain.

GOD AND OUR HISTORY

In asking for rain, we again remind God of his special relationship with us and our ancestors. We remind God of incidents in our common past which are tied in with water: the matriarch Rebecca was at a well when she came across Isaac's messenger, Moses struck a rock at God's command and water gushed out, Aaron and the Cohanim (priests) used water in the Temple rituals. And, of course, all the Jews were saved by the parting of the Red Sea.

Remember the twelve tribes	זְכוֹר, שְׁנֵים עָשָׂר שְׁבָטִים.
that you sent across the parted waters.	שֶׁהֶעֱבַרְתָּ, בְּגִזְרַת מַיִם.
You sweetened the bitter waters for them.	שֶׁהִמְתַּקְתָּ לָמוֹ, מְרִירוּת מַיִם.
Their generations	תּוֹלְדוֹתָם,
spilled blood like water for you.	נִשְׁפַּךְ דָּמָם עָלֶיךָ, כַּמַּיִם.
Look, for water has overwhelmed our souls.	תֵּפֶן כִּי נַפְשֵׁנוּ, אָפְפוּ מָיִם.
For their sake give water.	בְּצִדְקָם חוֹן, חֲשַׁרַת מָיִם.
For you are Adonai our God,	שָׁאַתָּה הוּא, יְהֹוָה אֱלֹהֵינוּ
who causes the wind to blow and the rain to fall.	מַשִּׁיב הָרוּחַ, וּמוֹרִיד הַגָּשֶׁם.

Too much rain can be destructive. That is why the prayer ends with a few words emphasizing the nourishing nature of the rain that is prayed for.

For a blessing and not for a curse. Amen.	לִבְרָכָה, וְלֹא לִקְלָלָה. אָמֵן
For life and not for death. Amen.	לְחַיִּים וְלֹא לַמָּוֶת. אָמֵן
For abundance and not for famine. Amen.	לְשֹׂבַע, וְלֹא לְרָזוֹן. אָמֵן

PRAYER VOCABULARY

their generations	תּוֹלְדוֹתָם
wind	רוּחַ
rain	גֶּשֶׁם

שִׂמְחַת תּוֹרָה
SIMCHAT TORAH

Simchat Torah is one of the most joyous holidays in the Jewish calendar. Even its name, "Rejoicing in the Torah," indicates this. In the diaspora, Simchat Torah is usually celebrated the day after Shemini Atzeret. In Israel and in the Reform tradition, Shemini Atzeret and Simchat Torah are celebrated on the same day.

THE YEARLY TORAH READING

Simchat Torah is a celebration of the end of one yearly cycle of readings from the Torah and the beginning of the next. In some places, the reading of the Torah is spread out over three years. However, the cycle is often limited to one year of set readings (*parashot*) spread out over the Shabbats of the year. The parashah for Simchat Torah is the last one of the Book of Deuteronomy, known as *Devarim* in Hebrew. In order to show that one is rejoicing not only to have finished the Torah, but also to be beginning it again, it became traditional at a very early date to include the first chapter of Genesis בְּרֵאשִׁית in the reading for this day.

CELEBRATING THE COMPLETION

In a celebration which includes both old and young, the Torah is paraded around the sanctuary (and sometimes in the street outside!) seven times. This is accompanied by joyful dancing and singing. Some Simchat Torah celebrations last for hours!

THE LAST PARASHAH

The last parashah of Devarim is called וְזֹאת הַבְּרָכָה , "this is the blessing." It ends the story of the Torah and of Moses. The Israelites are left on the verge of entering the promised land, and Moses gives them his final blessing and dies.

MOSES' BLESSING

The first part of the parashah contains the blessing of Moses. In it he blessed most of the tribes of Israel individually. At the end of the string of blessings he exulted:

O happy Israel!	אַשְׁרֶיךָ יִשְׂרָאֵל!
Who is like you,	מִי כָמוֹךָ,
a people saved by Adonai!	עַם נוֹשַׁע בַּיהוָֹה

[Deut 33:29a]

AND THE LAST SECTION

The last section of Devarim tell of the death of Moses and of the choosing of his successor, Joshua, who was to be the one to lead the Israelites into their home after forty years of wandering in the desert since their flight from Egypt.

Then Moses went up	וַיַּעַל מֹשֶׁה
from the desert of Moab	מֵעַרְבֹת מוֹאָב
to Mount Nebo, the summit of Pisgah,	אֶל־הַר נְבוֹ רֹאשׁ הַפִּסְגָּה,
which faces Jericho;	אֲשֶׁר עַל־פְּנֵי יְרֵחוֹ
and Adonai showed him all the land.	וַיַּרְאֵהוּ יְהוָֹה אֶת־כָּל־הָאָרֶץ.

[Deut 34:1a]

PRAYER VOCABULARY	
like you	כָמוֹךָ
a people	עַם
from the desert	מֵעַרְבֹת
all the land	כָּל־הָאָרֶץ

68

What follows is a description of the various regions of the land. After showing Moses the great expanse of land which he was never himself to enter, God described it to him:

This is the land which I promised   זֹאת הָאָרֶץ אֲשֶׁר נִשְׁבַּעְתִּי
   to Abraham, to Isaac, and to Jacob, saying: לְאַבְרָהָם לְיִצְחָק וּלְיַעֲקֹב לֵאמֹר

     I will give it to your descendants! לְזַרְעֲךָ אֶתְּנֶנָּה!

     I have let you see it with your own eyes, הֶרְאִיתִיךָ בְעֵינֶיךָ,

     but you yourself will never cross over there. וְשָׁמָּה לֹא תַעֲבֹר.

MOSES DIES

And so Moses the servant of Adonai died וַיָּמָת שָׁם מֹשֶׁה עֶבֶד־יְהֹוָה,

     there,

       in the land of Moab בְּאֶרֶץ מוֹאָב

         at the command of Adonai. עַל־פִּי יְהֹוָה

   And he buried him in the valley in the land וַיִּקְבֹּר אֹתוֹ בַגַּי

     of Moab, בְּאֶרֶץ מוֹאָב,

       opposite Bet Peor. מוּל בֵּית פְּעוֹר.

   No one knows his burial place, וְלֹא־יָדַע אִישׁ אֶת־קְבֻרָתוֹ,

     until this very day! עַד הַיּוֹם הַזֶּה:

[Deut 34:4b–6]

PRAYER VOCABULARY

I promised	נִשְׁבַּעְתִּי	and he buried	וַיִּקְבֹּר
to your descendents	לְזַרְעֲךָ	in the valley	בַגַּי
with your own eyes	בְעֵינֶיךָ	his burial place	קְבֻרָתוֹ
servant	עֶבֶד		

According to Jewish tradition, the reason that no one was allowed to find out where Moses was buried was so that no one would be tempted to worship him. After all, even though Moses was one of the greatest Jews of all time, if not the greatest, he was just a human being like everyone else. Like everyone else he had to obey God's laws; like so many others he died before he could finish his work. In order to avoid the sin of idolatry which would be caused by worshipping Moses, the place of his burial was left unknown. Yet the Bible does provide him with a most fitting epitaph, one which expresses his unique importance for the Jews as a lawgiver and a bringer of freedom:

MOSES AS PROPHET

No prophet has ever arisen in Israel to compare with Moses,

whom Adonai knew face-to-face..

וְלֹא־קָם נָבִיא עוֹד בְּיִשְׂרָאֵל
כְּמֹשֶׁה
אֲשֶׁר יְדָעוֹ יְהֹוָה פָּנִים אֶל־פָּנִים

[Deut 34:10]

A variation of this verse is found in the song Yigdal, which is often sung at the end of a service. Can you find it?

PRAYER VOCABULARY

prophet	נָבִיא
face to face	פָּנִים אֶל־פָּנִים

Focus on the Death of Moses

The traditional Jewish belief is that Moses personally wrote the Torah. This raises a problem. How can Moses have written about his own death? Rashi, the great medieval biblical interpreter, gives two possible answers. The first answer is that starting with the death of Moses, it was Joshua, Moses' successor, who continued the work of writing the Torah. The second answer is much more poignant. Moses wrote the Torah, word by word, as dictated by God. To be sure that he didn't make a mistake, Moses repeated the Torah, word by word, as he was writing. When God dictated the part about Moses' death, Moses continued to write but he did not repeat after God. While God dictated the passage about his coming death, Moses continued to write his words down, but with tears in his eyes.

70

CHATAN TORAH AND CHATAN BERESHIT

Being the person who reads the last part of Devarim or the one who reads the first part of Bereshit is considered to be a big honor. The former is traditionally called the *Chatan Torah*, the "bridegroom of the Torah," while the latter is referred to as the *Chatan Bereshit*, the "bridegroom of Genesis." Obviously these terms were coined at a time when women were not yet allowed to read from the Torah.

AND THE BEGINNING

Now that the cycle of readings from the Torah has ended with the end of Devarim, a symbolic start is made on the new cycle with the reading of the first story of creation in Bereshit, the first of the five books of the Torah.

CREATION

When God began to create	בְּרֵאשִׁית בָּרָא אֱלֹהִים
heaven and earth,	אֵת הַשָּׁמַיִם וְאֵת הָאָרֶץ,
—the earth being formless and void,	וְהָאָרֶץ הָיְתָה תֹהוּ וָבֹהוּ,
darkness was on the face of the deep,	וְחשֶׁךְ עַל־פְּנֵי תְהוֹם
and the breath of God hovered over the	וְרוּחַ אֱלֹהִים מְרַחֶפֶת
waters,	עַל־פְּנֵי הַמָּיִם.
God said, "Let there be light!"	וַיֹּאמֶר אֱלֹהִים "יְהִי אוֹר!"
And there was light.	וַיְהִי־אוֹר.
God saw that the light was good.	וַיַּרְא אֱלֹהִים אֶת־הָאוֹר כִּי־טוֹב.

PRAYER VOCABULARY

the heaven	הַשָּׁמַיִם
the earth	הָאָרֶץ
darkness	חשֶׁךְ
let there be light!	יְהִי אוֹר

This famous story of creation takes us through the six days of creation, when everything in the world was created by God, up to the seventh day, on which God rested and, in a manner of speaking, created Shabbat.

As the culmination of the six days of creation, God created humankind, both male and female. On the one hand the rabbis felt that human beings were created last as the culmination; on the other hand, lest we become too inflated about our own importance in the scheme of creation, the rabbis taught us to remember that the mosquito was created before us!

And God divided between the light	וַיַּבְדֵּל אֱלֹהִים בֵּין הָאוֹר
and the darkness.	וּבֵין הַחֹשֶׁךְ.
God called the light "day,"	וַיִּקְרָא אֱלֹהִים לָאוֹר "יוֹם,"
and the darkness he called "night."	וְלַחֹשֶׁךְ קָרָא "לָיְלָה"
There was evening,	וַיְהִי־עֶרֶב,
and there was morning.	וַיְהִי־בֹקֶר.
The first day!	יוֹם אֶחָד!

[Gen 1:1–5]

PRAYER VOCABULARY

day	יוֹם
night	לָיְלָה
evening	עֶרֶב
morning	בֹקֶר

72

Just as the ending of Devarim leads us into a new yearly cycle of readings from the Torah, which we begin by beginning Bereshit, so does the haftarah both begin and continue something.

The haftarah for Simchat Torah is the beginning of the Book of Joshua. At the end of Devarim, Moses had died just as the Israelites were about to enter the land which God had promised to them. The Book of Joshua, named after Moses' second-in-command and successor, continues the story of the Israelites and tells about how they came into the possession of their land, and about the fulfillment of God's promises.

After the death of Moses,	וַיְהִי אַחֲרֵי מוֹת מֹשֶׁה
the servant of Adonai,	עֶבֶד יְהֹוָה,
Adonai said to Joshua the son of Nun,	וַיֹּאמֶר יְהֹוָה אֶל־יְהוֹשֻׁעַ בִּן־נוּן
Moses' minister,	מְשָׁרֵת מֹשֶׁה,
"My servant Moses has died.	מֹשֶׁה עַבְדִּי מֵת.
Now, get up and cross this Jordan [River],	וְעַתָּה קוּם עֲבֹר אֶת־הַיַּרְדֵּן הַזֶּה
you and all of this people,	אַתָּה וְכָל־הָעָם הַזֶּה,
to the land which I am giving them,	אֶל־הָאָרֶץ אֲשֶׁר אָנֹכִי נֹתֵן לָהֶם,
to the children of Israel."	לִבְנֵי יִשְׂרָאֵל."

[Josh 1:1–2]

In this way, we are reminded that the Bible, and the story of God's involvement with the Jewish people, does not end with the Torah. From every ending, there is a new beginning!

PRAYER VOCABULARY

the death of	מוֹת	get up	קוּם
the servant	עֶבֶד	to the land	אֶל־הָאָרֶץ

73

PRAISE BEFORE THE ARK

The joyous nature of Simchat Torah is well known. In every congregation, there is much singing and dancing as all the Torah scrolls are paraded around the sanctuary. Children play an important role in the Simchat Torah celebration. They take part in the singing and dancing, often leading the way in the celebration with waving flags. All the children in the synagogue are also given an *aliyah* (עֲלִיָה) on Simchat Torah. This is the only time of year when children are honored by being called up to the Torah.

The fun of Simchat Torah is intended to praise God and the Torah which God gave the Jews. This praise also has a serious side to it. Every time we open the Holy Ark and take out a Torah scroll, we praise God through prayer. Simchat Torah marks the completion of the reading of the entire Torah. For this occasion there is a special prayer recited before the Torahs are carried throughout the synagogue.

This prayer is called the Ata Horeiyta (אַתָּה הָרְאֵתָ), which means "you have been shown," or "you have been taught." In reciting this prayer we are saying that through the Torah we have been taught about God.

The *Ata Horeiyta* prayer consists of verses from the Bible that describe the greatness of God, a quality which can only be learned from the Bible:

You have been taught to know	אַתָּה הָרְאֵתָ לָדַעַת
That Adonai is God.	כִּי יְהֹוָה הוּא הָאֱלֹהִים.
There is none other than him.	אֵין עוֹד מִלְּבַדּוֹ.
He alone does wondrous deeds,	לְעֹשֵׂה נִפְלָאוֹת גְּדֹלוֹת לְבַדּוֹ
for his lovingkindness is eternal.	כִּי לְעוֹלָם חַסְדּוֹ.

After this description, still using biblical phrases, we praise God:

There is none like you among the divine,	אֵין כָּמוֹךָ בָאֱלֹהִים,
Adonai,	אֲדֹנָי,
And there are no deeds such as yours.	וְאֵין כְּמַעֲשֶׂיךָ.
May Adonai's glory be eternal.	יְהִי כְבוֹד יְהֹוָה לְעוֹלָם.
May Adonai rejoice in his deeds.	יִשְׂמַח יְהֹוָה בְּמַעֲשָׂיו.
May Adonai's name be praised	יְהִי שֵׁם יְהֹוָה מְבֹרָךְ,
now and forever.	מֵעַתָּה וְעַד עוֹלָם.

Next, we ask for God's protection:

May Adonai our God be with us	יְהִי יְהֹוָה אֱלֹהֵינוּ עִמָּנוּ
As he was with our ancestors.	כַּאֲשֶׁר הָיָה עִם אֲבוֹתֵינוּ.
May he not leave us nor forsake us.	אַל יַעַזְבֵנוּ וְאַל יִטְּשֵׁנוּ.
Say: "Save us Adonai, our redeemer."	וְאִמְרוּ: "הוֹשִׁיעֵנוּ, אֱלֹהֵי יִשְׁעֵנוּ."

We then explain why we want to be saved:

To thank your holy name,
לְהוֹדוֹת לְשֵׁם קָדְשֶׁךָ,

    To be exalted in your song of praise.
לְהִשְׁתַּבֵּחַ בִּתְהִלָּתֶךָ.

Finally, the thoughts of this prayer are summarized in phrases which are familiar from other prayers which we have recited during the course of the year:

Adonai is king,
יְהֹוָה מֶלֶךְ,

    Adonai ruled,
יְהֹוָה מָלָךְ,

    Adonai will rule forever and ever.
יְהֹוָה יִמְלֹךְ לְעוֹלָם וָעֶד.

Adonai will give strength to his people,
יְהֹוָה, עֹז לְעַמּוֹ יִתֵּן,

    Adonai will bless his people with peace.
יְהֹוָה יְבָרֵךְ אֶת עַמּוֹ בַשָּׁלוֹם.

After this prayer is recited, the Hakafot, the processions with the Torah scrolls, begin. The familiar joy of Simchat Torah is well under way.

PRAYER VOCABULARY			
you have been taught	אַתָּה הָרְאֵתָ	our ancestors	אֲבוֹתֵינוּ
wondrous deeds	נִפְלָאוֹת גְּדֹלוֹת	save us	הוֹשִׁיעֵנוּ
his lovingkindness	חַסְדּוֹ	in your song of praise	בִּתְהִלָּתֶךָ
like you	כָּמוֹךָ	strength to his people	עֹז לְעַמּוֹ
in his deeds	בְּמַעֲשָׂיו	with peace	בַשָּׁלוֹם
with us	עִמָּנוּ		

Focus on Teaching and Learning

The Torah is often referred to as the "five books of Moses," or the "first five books of the Bible." The Torah is more than that. The word תּוֹרָה means "teaching." It has the same·root as the word מוֹרֶה ("teacher"). The Torah is the basic text for learning how to be a Jew. Most Jewish customs and concepts can be traced back to the Torah. Some of these may not appear to have a direct link, and different Jews may learn different things from the same Torah. Still, all Jewish learning is rooted in this Jewish teaching known as the Torah.

Focus on Two Special Honors

Besides the children's aliyah, there are two other aliyot unique to Simchat Torah. Both these aliyot have to do with the fact that we complete reading the Torah on Simchat Torah, and immediately begin reading it again. These two aliyot are considered to be very high honors. The first is called the *Chatan Torah* (חֲתָן תּוֹרָה), the bridegroom of the Torah. This is the aliyah for the last portion of the Torah. The second honor is called the *Chatan Bereshit* (חֲתָן בְּרֵאשִׁית), the bridegroom of Genesis. This aliyah is for the first portion of the Book of Genesis that is read. Notice that both honors are called "bridegrooms." This is because the Torah is thought of in the feminine, as the bride.

TWO MIDWINTER BREAKS

Simchat Torah marks the end of a hectic cycle of Jewish holidays in the fall. When it is over, the Jewish calendar is somewhat quiet. The winter season is broken up by two minor holidays, Chanukah and Tu BiShevat.

These are called minor holidays for a number of reasons. Both these festivals entered the Jewish calendar at a relatively late period. They are not as important as the other holidays we celebrate. For one thing, it is permissible to work during these days. This is not true of major holidays such as Yom Kippur or the first and last days of Pesach. Because they are minor holidays, there aren't many prayers associated with these two midwinter breaks.

חֲנֻכָּה
CHANUKAH: WINTER LIGHTS

The holiday of Chanukah begins on the twenty-fifth of Kislev and lasts for eight days. The word *Chanukah* means "dedication" in Hebrew. The festival commemorates the rededication of the Holy Temple in Jerusalem by the Maccabees in 165 B.C.E. The province of Judea and the Temple had fallen into the hands of the Hellenistic ruler Antiochus a few years earlier. Judah Maccabee and his brothers fought this Greek ruler. Tradition tells us that when they captured the Temple and tried to kindle the oil lamp there, they only found enough oil to last for one day. Miraculously, the lamp burned for eight days on this single day's supply. To commemorate this, we light up to eight candles on Chanukah.

MAOZ TSUR

The liturgy used on Chanukah developed relatively late in Jewish history. The most famous liturgical piece is a hymn called Maoz Tsur. This title is usually translated as "Rock of Ages," but this is somewhat incorrect. *Maoz* means "fortress," *tsur* is Hebrew for "rock." This hymn is believed to have been written in Germany in the thirteenth century. All we know about its author is his name—Mordechai. We know this because his name appears as an acrostic in the hymn. If you take the first letter of each of the five stanzas of Maoz Tsur, it will spell Mordechai in Hebrew.

Maoz Tsur is sung every night of Chanukah after the candles are lit. This is done both at home and in the synagogue.

The song begins by praising God, who is called a "rock of salvation."

Fortress, Rock of my Salvation,	מָעוֹז, צוּר יְשׁוּעָתִי,
It is proper to praise you.	לְךָ נָאֶה לְשַׁבֵּחַ.

The rest of the first stanza of Maoz Tsur deals with the rebuilding of the Temple. As the Maccabees were able to save the Temple in their day, the author hoped for a rebuilt Temple in his day.

THE CONCLUSION

Restore my house of prayer	תִּכּוֹן בֵּית תְּפִלָּתִי,
Where we will offer you thanks,	וְשָׁם תּוֹדָה נְזַבֵּחַ,
At the time when you prepare to do away with	לְעֵת תָּכִין מַטְבֵּחַ,
The howling oppressor.	מִצָּר הַמְנַבֵּחַ.
Then I will find fulfillment in a song,	אָז אֶגְמֹר בְּשִׁיר,
a hymn of the rededication of the altar.	מִזְמוֹר חֲנֻכַּת הַמִּזְבֵּחַ.

The next four stanzas refer to the way God has redeemed Israel in the past. First of all, from Egyptian slavery (Pesach), then from Babylonian exile, thirdly from Persian rule (Purim), and finally from the Greeks, a direct reference to the story of Chanukah.

The original Maoz Tsur contains a sixth stanza asking for the redemption of Israel. The redemption was meant to be from whatever oppression was taking place at the time. In later times, the sixth stanza was replaced by other ones also calling for redemption from the oppression of the time. Usually these stanzas also called for divine vengeance against the enemies of the Jews.

Today, we sing only five stanzas of Maoz Tsur. We no longer feel it is necessary or right to ask for divine vengeance against anybody.

The popularity of Maoz Tsur spread very quickly in the Ashkenazi world. One measure of this is the fact that it was translated into English and other languages in poetic translations suitable for singing. In fact, in many congregations today, it is customary to sing all or part of the Maoz Tsur in English so that all the participants may understand and enjoy the hymn's significance for Chanukah.

PRAYER VOCABULARY

fortress	מָעוֹז	in a song	בְּשִׁיר
my Salvation	יְשׁוּעָתִי	rededication of the altar	חֲנֻכַּת הַמִּזְבֵּחַ
my house of prayer	בֵּית תְּפִלָּתִי	Rock of Ages	מָעוֹז צוּר·

Focus on Divine Vengeance

Maoz Tsur is not the only place in which one finds Jews asking God to punish their foes. Throughout history there have been Jewish prayers written with this theme in mind. These prayers were written at times when Jews were persecuted and endangered. The prayers come from many countries. What they have in common is that they ask God to avenge Jews who suffered and died at the hands of gentile rulers. While prayers asking God to do evil against another person may horrify us today, we must keep in mind that this was the only way our persecuted people had of venting their frustration, sorrow, and anger about the suffering that they were forced to endure.

ט״ו בִּשְׁבָט
TU BISHEVAT: NATURE'S NEW YEAR

While it is still the middle of winter in North America, signs of spring begin to be seen in Israel. It is at this time of year that the holiday of Tu BiShevat, the annual celebration of the renewal of nature after the harsh winter, is celebrated. The name Tu BiShevat means "the fifteenth day of the month of Shevat."

Tu BiShevat is also called the "New Year of Trees." By this time, the rain and cold weather have come to an end in Israel. Traditionally, it is believed that now is the time when the sap starts running through the trees again, awakening them to a new spring.

Historically, Tu BiShevat was an agricultural holiday. A tax which was placed on fruit was due on this day in ancient Israel. (Think of what the fifteenth day of another month, April, means to families in the United States.)

When the Jews were exiled from the land of Israel and scattered in the Diaspora, Tu BiShevat took on new meanings. It was a way of keeping in contact with the Land of Israel. It became a special mitzvah (commandment) to eat fruit on Tu BiShevat, especially fruit that came from the Land of Israel. Dates, figs, grapes, and

82

carob are all types of fruit associated with Israel. In different countries, other celebrations were added to the holiday. North African and Asian Jews even created a Tu Bishevat Seder, modeled after the Passover Seder. Special poems were written for Tu BiShevat. In some communities, people stayed up all night on Tu BiShevat reading selections from the Bible and Talmud. In modern Israel, it is customary for children to plant trees on Tu BiShevat.

Since it is a "minor" holiday, there are no special prayers or services for Tu BiShevat. There is, however, one custom which is universal on this holiday—eating fruit. To mark this special occasion, the following blessing over the fruit is recited:

Blessed are you, Adonai our God,	בָּרוּךְ אַתָּה יְהֹוָה, אֱלֹהֵינוּ,
Ruler of the universe,	מֶלֶךְ הָעוֹלָם,
Creator of the fruit of the tree.	בּוֹרֵא פְּרִי הָעֵץ.

As on all other special occasions, such as lighting the candles on the first night of Chanukah, or the first Rosh Hashanah Kiddush, this blessing is followed by the *Shehechiyanu*:

Blessed are you, Adonai our God,	בָּרוּךְ אַתָּה יְהֹוָה, אֱלֹהֵינוּ
Ruler of the universe,	מֶלֶךְ הָעוֹלָם,
who has kept us alive and well	שֶׁהֶחֱיָנוּ וְקִיְּמָנוּ
and enabled us to	וְהִגִּיעָנוּ
celebrate this occasion.	לַזְּמַן הַזֶּה.

PRAYER VOCABULARY

fruit	פְּרִי
the tree	הָעֵץ

Focus on Hebrew Numbers

Every letter of the Hebrew alphabet also equals a number. Aleph is 1, bet is 2, and the counting continues until yod, the tenth letter. At this point the value of each letter jumps by ten: yod is 10, kaf is 20, until qof, which is 100. Now the counting proceeds by hundreds: qof equals 100, resh—200, shin—300, tav—400. In order to form other numbers, the different letters are put together in a word, and then the numerical value of each letter is added to the others in the word. For example, in this manner, adding yod (10) and aleph (1) would make 11. The name Tu BiShevat begins with the word made up of the letters tet (9) and vav (6). When 9 and 6 are added, the result is 15. That's how Tu BiShevat translates as "the fifteenth of Shevat." The reason that the letters yod (10) and he (5) are not combined to spell the number 15 is that they represent a way of writing God's name in Hebrew. The numbers of the Hebrew alphabet were taken very seriously by mystics. To them, the numerical value of Hebrew words was actually a secret code. The mystics tried to figure out the meaning of the code by relating words that had the same numerical value. This practice was known as Gematria, Jewish numerology.

ALEFBET NUMBER CHART

Name	Number	Letter	Name	Number	Letter	Name	Number	Letter	Name	Number	Letter
Alef	1	א	Het	8	ח	final Mem		ם	Tzadee	90	צ
Bet	2	ב	Tet	9	ט	Nun	50	נ	final Tzadee		ץ
Vet		ב	Yod	10	י	final Nun		ן	Kof	100	ק
Gimel	3	ג	Kaf	20	כ	Sameh	60	ס	Resh	200	ר
Dalet	4	ד	Haf		כ	Ayin	70	ע	Shin	300	ש
Hay	5	ה	final Haf		ך	Pay	80	פ	Sin		ש
Vav	6	ו	Lamed	30	ל	Fay		פ	Tav	400	ת
Zayin	7	ז	Mem	40	מ	final Fay		ף	Tav		ת

PURIM פּוּרִים
THE STORY OF ESTHER
ANYTHING GOES

PURIM AND THE MEGILLAH

The story of Purim is one that is probably familiar to everyone reading this book. Purim is a joyous holiday. There are few Jews who have not dressed up as Esther, Queen Vashti, King Ahasuerus, Mordechai, or Haman. The wild antics in the synagogue, and the noise whenever the name of . . . well, you know who . . . is mentioned make Purim an event that is looked forward to by young and old. The central event of the holiday is the public reading of the *Megillah*, the scroll of Esther.

You have already learned that there are five megillot that are read in the synagogue during the course of the Jewish year. However, there is only one that we refer to as *the* Megillah. This is *Megillat Esther* (מְגִילַת אֶסְתֵּר), which has long held a special place in Jewish hearts.

BOOKS ON SCROLLS

In ancient times, people did not write books as we know them. Books were made out of pieces of parchment, or leather, sewn together and rolled around two sticks. For most of us, the five books of the Torah are the only books that we come into contact with that are still written and read in this manner. That is, except for the Megillah. Throughout Jewish history, much of the greatest artistic talent of Jewish artists has been spent in writing *and* illustrating beautiful Megillot, which express the joy and energy of the holiday of Purim.

The basic story of Purim is simple: the Jewish people are saved by the valor of a Jewish woman, who ultimately assumes heroic dimensions when her people is threatened. However, the Scroll of Esther doesn't start by telling about Esther. First, it has to give us some background information in order to tell us how Esther got to be in a position to help save the Jews.

In the third year of his reign, King Ahasuerus of Persia gave a great feast for all of his nobles in Shushan, the capital. According to the Megillah, the feast lasted for 180 days! At the end of that time, when he was quite drunk, Ahasuerus wanted to show off how great he was. Since he had already shown everyone what kind of party he could throw, his palace and his riches, he decided to show his nobles his beautiful wife, Queen Vashti. She, however, refused to be exhibited to this drunken gathering. So, in a fit of anger, the king had her removed from being queen.

After all this had taken place, King Ahasuerus realized that he had been left without a queen. As we already know, having a beautiful queen was very important to Ahasuerus. So, on the advice of his nobles, Ahasuerus decided to hold a beauty contest for all young women in his kingdom to find the most beautiful one.

Focus on Vashti

When reading the story of Esther from a modern perspective, Vashti seems justified in refusing to appear before the king. Ahasuerus wanted to show off her beauty to men who had no right to see her exposed in this way. It is easy to understand Vashti's refusal and to sympathize with her plight. Yet in traditional Jewish belief, Vashti is not a figure to be pitied. In the Midrash, the rabbis tell many tales about her cruelty. She forced Jewish women to work on Shabbat. Vashti refused to appear before the king not out of modesty but out of shame because she had been struck with leprosy. According to the Midrash, God had Ahasuerus put Vashti to death for keeping the king from rebuilding the Temple in Jerusalem. Why is Vashti made out to be so cruel in the Midrash? There is no evidence for this cruelty in the Scroll of Esther. The probable reason is to contrast Vashti with Esther. The worse Vashti looks, the better Esther appears. Since Esther is the heroine of the story, the rabbis wanted to take no chances with any other character detracting from Esther's importance.

At this point the story leaves us hanging for a few lines, in order to introduce a couple of people who will be playing a most important role in the rest of the tale. It seems that living in Shushan at that time was a certain Jew named Mordechai, of the tribe of Benjamin, whose family had been exiled from Jerusalem by Nebuchadnezzar. Now, Mordechai had adopted his cousin Hadassah and raised her as his own daughter. Since Hadassah was both beautiful and, as we shall see, good, she was entered into the contest for queen. Like many Jews today, Hadassah had both a Hebrew name and a secular name. We know her best by her Babylonian name: Esther.

Focus on Names

As human beings travel from one culture to another, they enrich each other in many different ways. One of the truly fascinating, and for many people least understood, aspects of cultural cross-pollination is in our basic means of communication, the languages that we speak. If you were to investigate where the English language comes from, you would find that it is a mixture of mainly German and French elements, with a lot of Latin, Greek, and even Hebrew and Arabic words thrown in (not to mention many other languages, such as Spanish, which is having the biggest influence on English today). Some of the most common English names, such as David, Michael, Joseph, Samuel, Deborah, Ann (Hannah), and Judith, all entered English from Hebrew! These are all good Hebrew names! Yet not everything that we call a Hebrew name is actually Hebrew. Names also entered Hebrew and the Jewish community from other languages. For instance, Mendel, Zelig, Golda, and Freida all come from Yiddish (Jewish-German). Even names found in the Bible can be from other cultures among whom the Jews lived. From the period of slavery in Egypt come Pinehas (Phineas) and even the name of the greatest Jew of all time, Moses! From the period of the Exile in Babylon come the names Esther and Mordechai, which can be traced to the Babylonian divine names Ishtar and Marduk. Although most parents give their children a Jewish name, that name is not always originally Hebrew.

Around this time, Mordechai overheard two of the king's servants plotting against him. Mordechai told Esther about the plot, and Esther told Ahasuerus. When the report was investigated, it was found to be true. The plotters were executed, and Mordechai's good deed was recorded in the king's official records.

HAMAN AND THE JEWS

Meanwhile, the king had promoted one of his nobles, Haman the son of Hammedata the Agagite. Haman became the number two man in the kingdom. When Haman passed by, everyone had to bow down to him. However, there was one man who refused to bow down to him. That man was Mordechai. Haman was furious and decided to get rid of Mordechai. But when Haman found out that Mordechai was a Jew, he decided to try and kill *all* the Jews in Persia. Since most people at that time believed in omens, Haman cast lots in order to find a good day for killing the Jews. These lots were known in Persian as *purim*, from which we get the name of the holiday. The day that he decided on was in the twelfth month, the month of Adar.

Focus on Why Haman Hated the Jews

According to the Midrash, a clue to the question of why Haman hated the Jews is to be found in his name. He is called the "Agagite," that is to say a member of the family of Agag. Agag was a king of the Amalekites, the most ancient and most bitter enemies of the Jews according to the Bible. Agag and the Amalekites were defeated by Saul, the first king of the Jews. Saul was a member of the tribe of Benjamin, and therefore an ancestor of Mordechai. Thus the hatred between Haman and his people, and Mordechai and his people had ancient roots, which the centuries between the time of Saul and Agag, and Mordechai and Haman had not managed to erase.

After a year of preparation, Esther came before the king.

Esther was brought	וַתִּלָּקַח אֶסְתֵּר
to King Ahasuerus,	אֶל־הַמֶּלֶךְ אֲחַשְׁוֵרוֹשׁ,
to his royal house,	אֶל־בֵּית מַלְכוּתוֹ,
in the tenth month,	בַּחֹדֶשׁ הָעֲשִׂירִי
that is the month of Tevet,	הוּא־חֹדֶשׁ טֵבֵת,
in the seventh year of his reign.	בִּשְׁנַת־שֶׁבַע לְמַלְכוּתוֹ.
And the king loved Esther	וַיֶּאֱהַב הַמֶּלֶךְ אֶת־אֶסְתֵּר
more than any other woman.	מִכָּל־הַנָּשִׁים.
For she had found favor and esteem	וַתִּשָּׂא־חֵן וָחֶסֶד
before him,	לְפָנָיו,
more than any other young woman.	מִכָּל־הַבְּתוּלוֹת.
So he placed the royal crown on her head,	וַיָּשֶׂם כֶּתֶר־מַלְכוּת בְּרֹאשָׁהּ
and made her queen in place of Vashti.	וַיַּמְלִיכֶהָ תַּחַת וַשְׁתִּי.

THE FEAST

Then the king made a great feast	וַיַּעַשׂ הַמֶּלֶךְ מִשְׁתֶּה גָדוֹל
for all of his nobles and servants:	לְכָל־שָׂרָיו וַעֲבָדָיו:
the Feast of Esther.	אֵת מִשְׁתֵּה אֶסְתֵּר.

[Esth 2:16–18a]

So Esther became the queen of Persia, but, cautioned by Mordechai, she did not reveal to anyone that she was Jewish.

PRAYER VOCABULARY

of his reign	לְמַלְכוּתוֹ	a feast	מִשְׁתֶּה
women	נָשִׁים	his nobles	שָׂרָיו
young women	בְּתוּלוֹת	his servants	וַעֲבָדָיו
royal crown	כֶּתֶר־מַלְכוּת		

However, Haman still needed the king's permission for the deed:

So Haman said to King Ahasuerus:	וַיֹּאמֶר הָמָן לַמֶּלֶךְ אֲחַשְׁוֵרוֹשׁ:
"There is a certain people,	"יֶשְׁנוֹ עַם־אֶחָד,
scattered and dispersed	מְפֻזָּר וּמְפֹרָד
among the peoples,	בֵּין הָעַמִּים,
in all the states of your kingdom.	בְּכֹל מְדִינוֹת מַלְכוּתֶךָ.
Their laws are different	וְדָתֵיהֶם שֹׁנוֹת
from those of every other people,	מִכָּל־עָם,
and they don't obey the laws of the king.	וְאֶת־דָּתֵי הַמֶּלֶךְ אֵינָם עֹשִׂים.
It isn't in the king's interest to tolerate them."	וְלַמֶּלֶךְ אֵין שֹׁוֶה לְהַנִּיחָם."

[Esth 3:8]

With these bigoted words, and the payment of a bribe, Haman convinced the king to get rid of this troublesome people, *without* telling him who they were! The orders to kill the Jews were duly written and sealed with the king's signet-ring.

THE JEWS' REACTION

When the orders were posted throughout the Persian empire, there was mourning among all Jews. They tore their clothes and

PRAYER VOCABULARY

a certain people	עַם־אֶחָד	their laws	דָתֵיהֶם
scattered	מְפֻזָּר	the laws of the king	דָּתֵי הַמֶּלֶךְ
and dispersed	וּמְפֹרָד		

put on sackcloth and ashes. Even Mordechai was spotted near the palace in mourning by one of Esther's servants. Since Esther was living in the comfort of the palace, cut off from the world outside, she did not know about the planned destruction of her people. Mordechai's mourning surprised her. It wasn't until Mordechai pleaded with her to go to the king and beg him to cancel his orders that Esther heard about the troubles facing the Jews of Persia.

MORDECHAI GOES TO ESTHER

Mordechai knew that there was only one way to save the Jews, and that was to appeal to the king. And there was only one Jew who could approach the king, and that was Esther. However, Esther was afraid. After all, it had been thirty days since she had last been called in to Ahasuerus. Not only that, but she risked death by going in to the king unannounced. But Mordechai insisted.

"Don't expect	״אַל־תְּדַמִּי בְנַפְשֵׁךְ
to be the only Jew to escape,	לְהִמָּלֵט בֵּית־הַמֶּלֶךְ מִכָּל־הַיְּהוּדִים,
For if you remain silent at this time	כִּי אִם־הַחֲרֵשׁ תַּחֲרִישִׁי בָּעֵת הַזֹּאת.
relief and deliverance	רֶוַח וְהַצָּלָה
will come to the Jews	יַעֲמוֹד לַיְּהוּדִים
from some other place;	מִמָּקוֹם אַחֵר;
but you and your father's house will perish.	וְאַתְּ וּבֵית־אָבִיךְ תֹּאבֵדוּ.
Who knows if you weren't brought into	וּמִי יוֹדֵעַ אִם־לְעֵת כָּזֹאת הִגַּעַתְּ
the royal house just for this purpose?"	לַמַּלְכוּת.״

[Esth 4:13b–14]

PRAYER VOCABULARY

to escape	לְהִמָּלֵט	
relief	רֶוַח	

91

ESTHER GOES TO THE KING

Esther agreed to go in to the king, but only after Mordechai and all the rest of the Jews of Shushan had fasted for her for three days. On the third day, when Esther appeared before the king unannounced, Ahasuerus was happy to see her. He asked her what she wanted. Whatever it was, he would give it to her. All that Esther requested, however, was that Ahasuerus and Haman come to a private feast that she had prepared for them.

At the feast, the king again asked her what she wanted. Again, all that Esther requested was that Ahasuerus and Haman come to dine with her the following evening.

Haman left the feast in a good mood. After all, he had been the only one invited to dinner with the king and the queen. No one else in all the kingdom was as honored as he. Yet on his way out of the palace, he passed by Mordechai, who still wouldn't show him any respect. When he got home, he told his wife, family, and friends about his great honor. But as long as Mordechai was still alive, he could never be completely happy. So to cheer him up, his wife, Zeresh, suggested that he build a gallows for Mordechai, and go to the king in order to get his permission to hang him on it.

THE INSOMNIAC AHASUERUS

Meanwhile, the king had not been able to sleep. One of his servants read his official records to him. (That would probably manage to put anyone to sleep!) When he came to the account of the plot that Mordechai had reported, Ahasuerus asked what had been done to reward him. The answer was nothing. Just then, Haman arrived at the palace. The king asked him what he should do to someone whom he wanted to honor. Haman, thinking that the king must mean that he wanted to honor him, said that the person should be dressed in royal clothes, mounted on the king's horse, and led through the city by a noble who would call out:

"This is what the king does ּ כָּכָה יֵעָשֶׂה"

for the one he wants to honor!" לָאִישׁ אֲשֶׁר הַמֶּלֶךְ חָפֵץ בִּיקָרוֹ!"

[Esth 6:9b]

Ahasuerus liked Haman's suggestion. So he sent Haman out to do just that for his enemy, Mordechai. Poor Haman! He had barely gotten home in a bad mood when it was already time to rush off to dine with the king and the queen.

ESTHER APPEALS TO AHASUERUS

This time at dinner, Esther told Ahasuerus what she wanted, and what was bothering her. There was a certain evil man who wanted to harm her and her people. If he had only wanted to sell them into slavery, she wouldn't have complained. But since he wanted to kill her and her people, she had to appeal to the king. Ahasuerus was naturally very upset. Who dared to do that to his queen? The queen pointed at Haman the Agagite. Ahasuerus was so upset that he went into the garden to calm down. While he was gone, Haman became so frantic that he threw himself at Esther in order to beg for his life. When Ahauserus returned, he found Haman on Esther's couch. As if everything else that Haman had done wasn't bad enough, it now looked as if Haman were trying to molest the queen! Ahasuerus ordered Haman taken away and hung on the very gallows that he had built for Mordechai. The Jews were saved!

THE CELEBRATION

The rest of the scroll tells about how Mordechai took over Haman's place at court, how the Jews defended themselves against the people who tried to carry out Haman's plan to kill all of them, and how the Jews throughout Persia were commanded to observe the thirteenth and fourteenth days of Adar as a holiday in celebration of their rescue from destruction:

To make them days of feasting and joy, לַעֲשׂוֹת אוֹתָם יְמֵי מִשְׁתֶּה וְשִׂמְחָה

of sending gifts to one another, וּמִשְׁלֹחַ מָנוֹת אִישׁ לְרֵעֵהוּ

and gifts to the poor. וּמַתָּנוֹת לָאֶבְיוֹנִים.

PRAYER VOCABULARY			
feasting	מִשְׁתֶּה	gifts	מַתָּנוֹת
and joy	וְשִׂמְחָה	to the poor	לָאֶבְיוֹנִים
and sending gifts	מִשְׁלֹחַ מָנוֹת	Scroll of Esther	מְגִילַת אֶסְתֵּר

94

In many ways, Esther is one of the strangest books of the Bible. First of all, it is one of only two books in the Bible in which God is not mentioned at all! Shir Hashirim is the other one. The Bible is a religious work. But at first glance, there doesn't appear to be any religious element to the Scroll of Esther. Second, many people find its graphic depiction of the revenge that the Jews took on their enemies at the end of the Scroll offensive. Already in the Talmud, there can be found evidence of a controversy about including Esther in the Bible.

On the other hand, the great medieval scholar Moses Maimonides (1135–1204), known as the RaMBaM, following the Talmud, felt that Esther was the most important biblical book after the Torah. How could that be? Why has the Scroll of Esther been so popular among Jews for so many years?

Esther is the only book of the Bible which shows the most common problem facing Jews during the last two thousand years: living as a minority in an often unpredictably hostile world. Most of the world's Jews have lived, and many still do live, in countries like the Persia of Esther. These are countries in which the Jews live happiest when they are left alone as a group. Yet sometimes there arises someone like Haman, who, for no real reason, and helped by an uncaring government, can decide to try to kill all the Jews, or at least to limit their rights, just because they are different. Over the centuries this has happened to Jewish communities all over the world. Sometimes the Jews have escaped the danger, as in Esther's time. Sometimes they have not been so lucky, as in Europe between 1939 and 1945, when the Nazis and their allies, under the leadership of a modern Haman, killed six million Jews just because they were Jewish, as well as millions of other innocents.

Megillat Esther has given hope to Jews for over two thousand years that they will survive and overcome their enemies. The holiday of Purim, which is a joyous celebration, gains added significance for oppressed or fearful people. The gift of Megillat Esther to Jews has been one of the most precious, the gift of hope.

PURIM IN SONG

As we all know, the story of Purim gives Jews much cause for celebration. Throughout history, people have celebrated with song. This holds true in the Jewish tradition as well. Chanukah, another joyous holiday, is rich with songs familiar to all of us. Purim, too, has a wealth of songs.

If you were to write a Purim song, what would you write about? Your song might be about the hamentaschen we eat. Perhaps you like "graggers," the noisemakers used on Purim. You might even write about dressing up in a Purim costume. There are songs about all these things. One subject which you would probably consider is the story of Purim, the story read in Megillat Esther, the Scroll of Esther. It isn't surprising, then, that such a song exists. This song which summarizes the Purim story is called *Shoshanat Ya'akov* (שׁוֹשַׁנַת יַעֲקֹב) "the Flower of Jacob." This name refers to the Jewish people.

Focus on Nicknames for the Jewish People

Shoshanat Ya'akov sounds like a silly thing to call the Jews. The Jacob part is easy to understand. Jacob was the forefather who changed his name to Israel. The Jews are referred to as the *b'nai yisrael,* "the children of Israel." Another nickname for the Jews is the "chosen people." Still another name is "the people of the book." Why compare the Jews to a flower? Perhaps there is a wish in the name Shoshanat Ya'akov, the hope that the Jewish people will continue to "flower." Finally, Shoshanat Ya'akov is also a pun. After all, the events of Purim take place in the city of Shushan. It is the Jews of this city who are refered to as the Shoshanah, the flower.

The song Shoshanat Ya'akov tells the part of the Purim tale worth singing about, how Mordechai won and Haman lost the political battle, and how the Jews were saved:

The "Shushan Jews" (flower of Jacob)   שׁוֹשַׁנַּת יַעֲקֹב

    shouted with joy   צָהֲלָה וְשָׂמֵחָה

    when they saw Mordechai dressed in   בִּרְאוֹתָם יַחַד תְּכֵלֶת

        royal purple.   מָרְדְּכָי.

The song then thanks God for having saved the Jews:

You were always their salvation   תְּשׁוּעָתָם הָיִיתָ לָנֶצַח

    and their hope in every generation.   וְתִקְוָתָם בְּכָל דּוֹר וָדוֹר.

To tell that those who have hope in you will   לְהוֹדִיעַ שֶׁכָּל קֹוֶיךָ לֹא

    not be shamed,   יֵבוֹשׁוּ,

    those who seek refuge in you shall never   וְלֹא יִכָּלְמוּ לָנֶצַח כָּל

        be disappointed.   הַחוֹסִים בָּךְ.

Finally, using familiar phrases, the idea of Purim is stated in a nutshell:

Cursed is Haman   אָרוּר הָמָן

    who tried to make me perish.   אֲשֶׁר בִּקֵּשׁ לְאַבְּדִי,

    Praised is Mordechai the Jew.   בָּרוּךְ מָרְדְּכַי הַיְּהוּדִי.

PRAYER VOCABULARY

flower of Jacob	שׁוֹשַׁנַּת יַעֲקֹב	who seek refuge	הַחוֹסִים
their salvation	תְּשׁוּעָתָם	cursed is	אָרוּר
and their hope	וְתִקְוָתָם	praised is	בָּרוּךְ

קְרִיאַת הַתּוֹרָה לְפֶּסַח
PESACH:
THE TORAH PORTIONS

The major Torah portions for the first and last days of Pesach deal appropriately enough with the biblical story of the first Passover, the hurried Exodus from Egypt, and the miracle at the Reed Sea. In other words, these Torah portions relate the actual story of Pesach.

Two of the major symbols of Pesach are the paschal lamb and the matzah. Both of these play a role in the story.

THE DEATH OF THE FIRSTBORN

The Pesach Torah portions start with the preparations for the tenth and last plague, the death of the firstborn of Egypt. While the Angel of Death passed through Egypt, God commanded the Israelites to sacrifice a lamb and paint the doorframes of their homes with its blood, so that the Angel would know to pass over them. Meanwhile, they were to remain inside and eat a Passover meal, consisting of the sacrificed lamb.

As the Israelites remained safe in their homes, the Angel of Death passed through Egypt, killing all the firstborn in the land, from that of Pharaoh, to that of the prisoner in the dungeon, to the firstborn of the cattle. As a result of this destruction, the Egyptians finally let the Israelite slaves leave the land of their bondage. The Bible tells of their departure:

THE EXODUS

The Israelites traveled

  from Raamses to Sukkot,

    in all about 600,000 men,

      not counting children.

A great multitude also went up with them,

  as well as flocks and great herds of cattle.

וַיִּסְעוּ בְנֵי־יִשְׂרָאֵל

מֵרַעְמְסֵס סֻכֹּתָה,

כְּשֵׁשׁ־מֵאוֹת אֶלֶף רַגְלִי הַגְּבָרִים,

לְבַד מִטָּף.

וְגַם־עֵרֶב רַב עָלָה אִתָּם,

וְצֹאן וּבָקָר מִקְנֶה כָּבֵד מְאֹד.

THE DOUGH

They baked the dough,

  which they brought out of Egypt,

    into cakes of matzah, since it hadn't risen;

    since they were thrown out of Egypt,

    they were not able to delay,

    and they didn't even prepare any

      provisions for themselves.

וַיֹּאפוּ אֶת־הַבָּצֵק

אֲשֶׁר הוֹצִיאוּ

עֻגֹת כִּי לֹא חָמֵץ,

כִּי־גֹרְשׁוּ מִמִּצְרַיִם,

וְלֹא יָכְלוּ לְהִתְמַהְמֵהַּ,

וְגַם־צֵדָה לֹא־עָשׂוּ לָהֶם.

[Ex 12:37–39]

In this manner, the matzah became a symbol and remembrance of the quickly cooked bread that the Israelites had to eat when they were thrown out of Egypt, just as the paschal lamb became a symbol for the lamb that was eaten on the night of the actual passing-over of the Angel of Death. Both are included in our Pesach meal.

PRAYER VOCABULARY

they baked	וַיֹּאפוּ	to delay	לְהִתְמַהְמֵהַּ
the dough	אֶת־הַבָּצֵק	provisions	צֵדָה
were thrown out	גֹרְשׁוּ		

99

As the Israelites made their escape, God guided them by means of a pillar of cloud by day, and a pillar of fire by night. However, the Egyptians began to regret letting them go, and Pharaoh went off with his army in pursuit of the Israelites.

AT BAY

Finally, the Israelites were cornered between the Egyptian army and the Reed Sea. They despaired of their chances of survival and turned against Moses. It was at this seemingly hopeless point that God's greatest act of deliverance took place.

THE SEA SPLITS

At God's command, Moses held his arm over the sea, the waters parted, and the Israelites marched over to safety on the other side. Out of Egypt at last! When the Egyptians tried to continue their pursuit of the Israelites across the passage through the sea, the waters closed in over them, and Pharaoh's army was destroyed.

According to later Jewish tradition, God would not allow the angels to rejoice in song at this time. "How can you sing Halleluyah when my creatures are dying?" he asked.

The Bible, however, only records the song of rejoicing that the Israelites sang at the Reed Sea:

Then Moses and the Israelites sang	אָז יָשִׁיר־מֹשֶׁה וּבְנֵי יִשְׂרָאֵל
this song to Adonai.	אֶת־הַשִּׁירָה הַזֹּאת לַיהוָה
they said:	וַיֹּאמְרוּ לֵאמֹר.
"Let me sing to Adonai,	"אָשִׁירָה לַיהוָה,
for he is greatly exalted.	כִּי־גָאֹה גָּאָה.
Horse and its rider	סוּס וְרֹכְבוֹ
he has cast into the sea!"	רָמָה בַיָּם!"

[Ex 15:1]

PRAYER VOCABULARY

this song	הַשִּׁירָה	and its rider	וְרֹכְבוֹ
let me sing	אָשִׁירָה	he has cast	רָמָה
horse	סוּס		

You are all probably familiar with the following quotation from the "Song of the Sea." Do you remember where you know it from?

Who is like you among the divine beings, מִי כָמֹכָה בָּאֵלִים, יְהֹוָה?
    Adonai?

Who is like you glorious in holiness, מִי כָּמֹכָה נֶאְדָּר בַּקֹּדֶשׁ,
    deserving of praises, נוֹרָא תְהִלֹּת,
        doing wonders? עֹשֵׂה־פֶלֶא?

[Ex 15:11]

PRAYER VOCABULARY

praises	תְהִלֹּת
wonders	פֶלֶא

At the end of this song, the Bible records how Miriam, the sister of Moses and Aaron, led the Israelite women in celebration:

Miriam the prophetess, the sister of Aaron, took וַתִּקַּח מִרְיָם הַנְּבִיאָה,

the timbrel in her hand, אֲחוֹת אַהֲרֹן, אֶת־הַתֹּף בְּיָדָהּ,

and all the women went out after her וַתֵּצֶאןָ כָל־הַנָּשִׁים אַחֲרֶיהָ

dancing with timbrels. בְּתֻפִּים וּבִמְחֹלֹת

And Miriam sang to them: וַתַּעַן לָהֶם מִרְיָם:

"Sing to Adonai. "שִׁירוּ לַיהוָה

For he is greatly exalted! כִּי־גָאֹה גָּאָה!

Horse and its rider סוּס וְרֹכְבוֹ

he has cast into the sea." רָמָה בַיָּם."

[Ex 15:20–21]

PRAYER VOCABULARY

the prophetess	הַנְּבִיאָה	horse	סוּס
timbrel	תֹּף	and its rider	וְרֹכְבוֹ
		into the sea	בַיָּם

הַהַגָּדָה
THE HAGGADAH:
TELLING THE PASSOVER STORY

THE PILGRIMAGE FESTIVALS

The Bible mentions five holidays. These are Rosh Hashanah, Yom Kippur, and the three pilgrimage festivals, *Shalosh Regalim*. They are called pilgrimage festivals because Jews were expected to travel to Jerusalem during these holidays. These three holidays are *Pesach*, *Shavuot*, and *Sukkot*. The pilgrimage festivals have some features in common. All three of them are associated with agriculture. Pesach is the time of the early spring harvest, Shavuot celebrates the barley harvest of midsummer, and Sukkot, the fall harvest. Two of these holidays (Pesach and Sukkot) last for a week.

Each of these holidays also has many other meanings as well. They all serve as reminders of important events in biblical history.

PESACH AND THE HAGGADAH

The historical events of Pesach are the most familiar of the Shalosh Regalim. This is due in large part to a popular book that has kept the meaning of Pesach fresh in the minds of all Jews. This book is the Haggadah.

הַגָּדָה is Hebrew for "telling." The Haggadah, read during the Passover *Seder,* is the yearly telling and reenactment of the story of the Exodus from Egypt. The Haggadah is a very old book that has had many portions added to it throughout Jewish history. When we read the Haggadah, we are reading the words of many Jewish authors scattered throughout different countries, over a period of more than one thousand years.

Although there are many different and creative versions of the Haggadah, each Haggadah begins by listing the order of the events that will take place at the Seder. As with the other two of the Shalosh Regalim, Pesach starts with a Kiddush for the specific holiday.

This is followed by the Shehechiyanu blessing thanking God for letting us celebrate the occasion.

Next in the order is the eating of a green vegetable. Some people believe that the green vegetable symbolizes the relation of Passover to the ancient early-spring harvest.

After this, a piece of matzah is broken and hidden for the *afikoman* (dessert).

Now comes the major part of the Seder, called the *maggid*, "telling" the story of Passover as written in the Haggadah.

The story begins with a short summary of what is going to take place. The summary is in Aramaic, which at one time was the most common language of the Jews. This Aramaic passage, called *Ha-Lachma Anya* ("this is the bread of affliction"), explains the central symbol and message of Pesach. Matzah is the bread of poverty eaten by our ancestors in Egypt. This year we act as though in slavery, next year we will all be free people.

Next comes the most familiar part of the Seder, the four questions. These questions ask what makes Passover different. Why do we eat matzah and bitter herbs? Why are we at a Seder?

PRAYER VOCABULARY

three pilgrimage festivals	שָׁלֹשׁ רְגָלִים	dessert/Afikoman	אֲפִיקוֹמָן
Haggadah	הַגָּדָה	telling/Maggid	מַגִּיד
order/Seder	סֵדֶר	bread of poverty	לֶחֶם עֹנִי

The rest of the Haggadah answers these questions. The first part of the answer is simple:

We were slaves to Pharaoh in Egypt.	עֲבָדִים הָיִינוּ לְפַרְעֹה בְּמִצְרָיִם.
But Adonai our God brought us out of there	וַיּוֹצִיאֵנוּ יְהֹוָה אֱלֹהֵינוּ מִשָּׁם
with a strong hand and outstretched arm.	בְּיָד חֲזָקָה וּבִזְרוֹעַ נְטוּיָה.
If the Holy One, praised be he,	וְאִלּוּ לֹא הוֹצִיא הַקָּדוֹשׁ בָּרוּךְ הוּא,
had not brought	
our ancestors out of Egypt,	אֶת־אֲבוֹתֵינוּ מִמִּצְרַיִם,
then we, our children, and their children	הֲרֵי אָנוּ וּבָנֵינוּ וּבְנֵי בָנֵינוּ
would still be enslaved to Pharaoh	מְשֻׁעְבָּדִים הָיִינוּ לְפַרְעֹה
in Egypt.	בְּמִצְרָיִם.

We are then told that it is our duty to tell the story of the Exodus throughout all our generations. In the telling lie the answers to the four questions. From here on the Haggadah does a number of things. It tells the story of the Exodus, provides commentaries on the story from a number of rabbis, and gives all types of aids for recounting and remembering the story. A good example of this is its handling of the ten plagues. The plagues listed in the Haggadah are taken from the biblical account.

PRAYER VOCABULARY

slaves	עֲבָדִים	our ancestors	אֲבוֹתֵינוּ
with a strong hand	בְּיָד חֲזָקָה	our children	בָּנֵינוּ
and outstretched arm	וּבִזְרֹעַ נְטוּיָה	be enslaved	מְשֻׁעְבָּדִים

Blood, frogs, lice, wild beasts, plague, דָּם. צְפַרְדֵּעַ. כִּנִּים. עָרוֹב דֶּבֶר.

boils, hail, locusts, darkness, שְׁחִין. בָּרָד. אַרְבֶּה חֹשֶׁךְ.

death of the firstborn. מַכַּת בְּכוֹרוֹת.

After the listing of the ten plagues, the Haggadah contains a shorthand method for remembering all the plagues in their correct order. Rabbi Yehuda came up with this method. It involves taking the first letter of each of the plagues and making three words out of the combined letters.

D'TZaKh ADaSH B'ACHaV   דְּצַ"ךְ עֲדַ"שׁ בְּאַחַ"ב:

PRAYER VOCABULARY

blood	דָּם	hail	בָּרָד
plague	דֶּבֶר	death of the firstborn	מַכַּת בְּכוֹרוֹת

Focus on Hebrew Abbreviations

All languages have different ways to abbreviate words. In English, for example, we usually shorten words such as titles. *President* becomes *Pres.*, doctor is *dr.* The Hebrew language abbreviates words in a different way. In fact, in Hebrew it is common to abbreviate phrases. This is done, as Rabbi Yehuda demonstrates above, by taking the initial letter of each word. The vowel *a* is added to help pronounce the abbreviation. One well-known Hebrew abbreviation is the word *TaNaKh*. It stands for *(T)orah, (N)evi'im, (K)etubim*. That is, Torah, Prophets, and Writings, the three sections of the Hebrew Bible. TaNaKh, therefore, is how you would say Bible in Hebrew. In English we have similar abbreviations, but they are not as common as in Hebrew. NASA is one such English abbreviation. Can you think of some more?

Thanks to Rabbi Yehuda, it is possible for us to remember all ten plagues in their proper order. Other rabbis provided us with various explanations of the plagues. We all know that there were ten plagues, but according to the commentary that is found in the Haggadah, the plagues may have numbered up to 250! How did they arrive at this number? The rabbis read the story of the Exodus very carefully. Each word was considered important. At one point in the Exodus story, Pharaoh's people say that the plague is the *finger* of God. Later in the story, at the crossing of the Reed Sea, it says that Israel saw the strong *hand* of God. The rabbis thought the use of finger and hand was significant. They figured out that if one finger equaled ten plagues, a hand, or five fingers, equaled fifty plagues. Other rabbis in reading the story found other significant words in it. Through commenting on these words and using simple arithmetic, it finally reached the point that Rabbi Akiva was able to show that there had been 250 plagues against the Egyptians! He got this number by multiplying the five terms for anger used in the Bible by the ten plagues, and then by the five fingers on God's hand at the Reed Sea ($5 \times 10 \times 5 = 250$).

The rabbis did not provide such commentary merely to enhance the story of Pesach. Their most important contribution was setting guidelines for what must take place at the Seder. The earliest Seder consisted of eating the paschal (Passover) lamb, matzah, and bitter herbs, and drinking four cups of wine. The oldest part of the Haggadah tells us that these symbols are an essential part of the Seder.

Rabban [Rabbi] Gamliel would say,   רַבָּן גַּמְלִיאֵל הָיָה אוֹמֵר.

"All who do not say these three things   כָּל שֶׁלֹּא אָמַר שְׁלֹשָׁה דְבָרִים אֵלוּ

on Pesach have not fulfilled their duty.   בַּפֶּסַח, לֹא יָצָא יְדֵי חוֹבָתוֹ.

And these are the things: וְאֵלּוּ הֵן:

    The paschal offering, matzah,   פֶּסַח. מַצָּה.

       and bitter herbs."   וּמָרוֹר.

     Not only did Rabbi Gamliel provide instructions for the Seder, he even provided the words to explain what each item means.

THE PASCHAL LAMB

The paschal lamb which our ancestors ate   פֶּסַח שֶׁהָיוּ אֲבוֹתֵינוּ אוֹכְלִים

    when the Temple existed,   בִּזְמַן שֶׁבֵּית הַמִּקְדָּשׁ הָיָה קַיָּם,

    what is the reason for it?   עַל שׁוּם מָה?

The reason was that the Holy One,   עַל שׁוּם שֶׁפָּסַח הַקָּדוֹשׁ

    blessed be he, passed over the houses   בָּרוּךְ הוּא, עַל בָּתֵּי

    of our ancestors in Egypt.   אֲבוֹתֵינוּ בְּמִצְרַיִם.

PRAYER VOCABULARY

the paschal offering	פֶּסַח	the Temple	בֵּית הַמִּקְדָּשׁ
matzah	מַצָּה	passed over	פָּסַח
and bitter herbs	וּמָרוֹר	the houses of	בָּתֵּי

THE MATZAH

The matzah which we eat,

what is the reason for it?

The reason is that there was not

enough time for the dough of our ancestors

[in Egypt] to become leavened.

מַצָּה זוֹ שֶׁאָנוּ אוֹכְלִים,

עַל שׁוּם מָה?

עַל שׁוּם שֶׁלֹּא הִסְפִּיק

בְּצֵקָם שֶׁל אֲבוֹתֵינוּ

לְהַחֲמִיץ.

THE BITTER HERBS

The bitter herbs which we eat,

what is the reason for it?

The reason is that the Egyptians

made the lives of our ancestors

in Egypt bitter.

מָרוֹר זֶה שֶׁאָנוּ אוֹכְלִים,

עַל שׁוּם מָה?

עַל שׁוּם שֶׁמֵּרְרוּ הַמִּצְרִים

אֶת־חַיֵּי אֲבוֹתֵינוּ

בְּמִצְרָיִם.

These symbols are actually the oldest part of the Passover Seder. The story of the Exodus was added to enhance this. As time went by, other customs, used by different rabbis, were also included. For example, we eat bitter herbs and matzah together because this is what Hillel did. Later, commentaries on these customs and on the Exodus story were added to the central ceremony. Throughout the centuries, Jews have been making additions to the Haggadah.

PRAYER VOCABULARY	
their dough	בְּצֵקָם
to become leavened	לְהַחֲמִיץ
the lives of	אֶת־חַיֵּי
our ancestors	אֲבוֹתֵינוּ

Many of the songs date to the Middle Ages. Some songs, such as *Dayenu*, summarize the story of the Exodus. Other songs, such as *Echad Mi Yodea* ("who knows one"), are meant for entertainment and to provide a review of basic Jewish knowledge.

Even today there are changes being made in the Haggadah. Some Haggadot contain special readings about the Holocaust. Others have selections dealing with the State of Israel. A number of Haggadot published in the United States include special American songs and symbols. Many modern Passover customs have arisen concerning Jews who are in lands, such as the Soviet Union, where they cannot live as free people. The Haggadah is a collection of works around the theme of freedom. Each generation of Jews has added its own thoughts on the subject to this collection. That is why the Haggadah has expanded so much over the centuries, and continues to change today. It is truly one of the best reflections of the state of world Jewry.

GETTING READY FOR THE SPRING HARVEST

Just as Sukkot celebrates the fall harvest, Passover celebrates the harvest of early spring. During Sukkot a prayer is introduced asking for rainfall. This prayer is recited during the *Amidah* prayer until the first day of Passover. At this time we no longer ask for rain. Rain is needed during the winter in the Land of Israel. During the spring, in order for plants to flourish, dew is necessary. For this reason, on the first day of Passover, we read a prayer asking for dew to nourish the earth.

Focus on Praying for the Weather

In asking for either rain or dew, depending on the season, the agricultural roots of many Jewish holidays become apparent. Since it was in the Land of Israel that Jews farmed in ancient times, these prayers associated with the weather are meant for farmers in Israel. Even after Jews were exiled, their prayers for rain and dew reflected their wishes for the harvest in Israel. Today, these prayers take on new meaning. Some people think of the produce of modern kibbutzim when they recite them. Other people say these prayers for farmers all over the world.

With dew you bless our food. טַל בּוֹ תְּבָרֵךְ מָזוֹן.

  May there not be leanness among our בְּמִשְׁמַנֵּינוּ אַל יְהִי רָזוֹן.

  fatted flock.

This people you have tended like sheep. אוּמָה אֲשֶׁר הִסַּעְתָּ כַצֹּאן.

Give them their desire—with dew. אָנָּא תָפֵק־לָהּ רָצוֹן. בְּטָל:

  For you are Adonai our God, שָׁאַתָּה הוּא יְהוָֹה אֱלֹהֵינוּ,

  who causes the wind to blow מַשִּׁיב הָרוּחַ

  and the dew to descend. וּמוֹרִיד הַטָּל.

For a blessing and not a curse. Amen לִבְרָכָה וְלֹא לִקְלָלָה, אָמֵן.

For life and not for death. Amen לְשׂוֹבַע וְלֹא לְרָזוֹן, אָמֵן.

For abundance and not for famine. Amen לְחַיִּים וְלֹא לְמָוֶת, אָמֵן.

At times, it may seem strange to us to be praying for rain or dew; after all, most of us do not farm. However, when we think of the food we eat and how much of it depends on good growing conditions, the importance of these prayers for all of us becomes clear.

PRAYER VOCABULARY

you bless	תְּבָרֵךְ
food	מָזוֹן
the wind	הָרוּחַ
for a blessing	לִבְרָכָה
for life	לְחַיִּים
for abundance	לְשׂוֹבַע

שִׁיר הַשִּׁירִים
SHIR HASHIRIM: A LOVE SONG FOR THE YOUNG YEAR

One of the most remarkable books in the Bible is the one called *Shir Hashirim*, the Song of Songs. According to Rabbi Akiva, who lived in Israel (Judea) in the early second century C.E., Shir Hashirim is the holiest book outside of the Torah. Yet it doesn't even mention God. It is traditionally considered to be morally most uplifting. Yet it contains the most romantic love poetry in biblical literature. A great deal has been written about this book. Yet it is one of the shortest books in the Bible. How can all this be?

Shir Hashirim holds a special place in Jewish tradition. Rabbi Akiva's evaluation has generally been accepted by Jews all over the world. Shir Hashirim is read in the synagogue ritual at two different times. First, on a weekly basis, it is read in some traditions as part of the Kabbalat Shabbat service welcoming the Sabbath. Second, it is read on the Shabbat of Pesach. At first glance, Shir Hashirim seems an unlikely choice for such religious devotion.

After a short introduction which ascribes the writing of the book to King Solomon, the book launches right into its main theme:

The Song of Songs of Solomon

שִׁיר הַשִּׁירִים אֲשֶׁר לִשְׁלֹמֹה:

[Shir 1:1]

May he kiss me with the kisses

of his mouth,

for your love is better than wine.

יִשָּׁקֵנִי מִשִּׁיקוֹת

פִּיהוּ

כִּי־טוֹבִים דֹּדֶיךָ מִיָּיִן.

[Shir 1:2]

PRAYER VOCABULARY			
song	שִׁיר	than wine	מִיָּיִן
may he kiss me	יִשָּׁקֵנִי		

Since most of its language is of a distinctly romantic nature, how could such a book find its way into the most sacred literature of the Jews?

THE AUTHOR

First of all, according to the tradition the book was written by Solomon. Solomon was famous for his many wise sayings and songs. The books of Proverbs and Kohelet were also supposed to have been written by him. According to the Midrash, Solomon wrote the love songs of Shir Hashirim when he was a young man, the wise sayings of Proverbs when he was in his middle age, and the reflective and cynical Book of Kohelet near the end of his long life. Since anything that Solomon said was supposedly divinely inspired, it is not difficult to see how any work felt to have been written by him was preserved as a part of the Jewish holy literature.

115

Second, the rabbis were able to transform the simple meaning of the text into a book describing the intimate relationship between God and the people of Israel by means of allegorical interpretation. An allegory is a story which seems to describe one thing, but is actually describing something else.

Focus on a Famous Allegory

One of the most famous allegories ever written can be found in the Bible, in the Second Book of Samuel, chapters 11–12. Like all biblical heroes, King David was human, that is to say he had his faults. Once he became king, he sometimes acted like a despot instead of a just ruler. David fell in love with Batsheva, the wife of Uriah. Since David wanted to marry Batsheva, he had Uriah killed "by accident" in a battle. No one knew or dared to criticize David, so he married Batsheva. However, God sent Nathan the prophet, who dared to speak in the name of the truth to David. Through the use of an allegory, Nathan was able to get David to accuse himself. Nathan told David a story about two men in a certain city, one rich, the other poor. The rich man had many sheep, but the poor man only had one little lamb, which was a treasured pet for him and his family. However, one day the rich man got a guest. But instead of taking one of the sheep from his many flocks, he took the poor man's lamb, slaughtered it, and gave it to his guest to eat. When he heard the story, David was furious at such an injustice being done in his kingdom. He demanded to know who the rich man was, in order to punish him. "You are the man!" was Nathan's shattering reply.

116

Rabbi Akiva, who felt that Shir Hashirim was such a holy book, was a person who believed in the allegorical interpretation of the book. He complained about the people who sang the lyrics of the Song at parties and in taverns. According to Rabbi Akiva and most other traditional interpreters of the book, there is nothing secular or vulgar about the language of Shir Hashirim.

Using the image of love and marriage, the book tried to convey the intimacy of the relationship between God and Israel, with God the husband, and Israel as the bride. It is in this sense that the book is read at Pesach. The reading of Shir Hashirim is symbolic of the courtship of God and Israel, prior to their marriage with the giving of the Torah at Mount Sinai at Shavuot time, seven weeks later.

Focus on Another Jewish Interpretation of Shir Hashirim

By the year 1492, when life in Jewish Spain came to an official end with the expulsion of the remaining Jews from Spain, the remnants of Spanish Jewry were scattered, from Holland in the west to the land of Israel in the east. In Israel, a colony of Jewish mystics was established in the Galilean mountain town of Safed (Tsefat). Over the next centuries, this was to be one of the centers of Jewish learning. The basic text of the Jewish mystical movement is the *Zohar*. According to Kabbalah, which is the name given to mystical Jewish teaching, God created a mate for each of the days of the week except Shabbat. Israel was therefore created to be Shabbat's husband. Every Friday evening, the mystics of Safed would go out into the fields to welcome Shabbat, the queen and bride. The song Lecha Dodi, "Come, my beloved, let us meet the bride," was written for this occasion. Shir Hashirim, the love song between Israel, the husband, and Shabbat, the bride, was also sung at this time. This latter custom continues in a number of synagogues down to this very day.

Most of the time it is a woman who is speaking of her love, but sometimes it is a man:

"Behold, you are beautiful, my beloved!   "הִנָּךְ יָפָה, רַעְיָתִי!

Behold, you are beautiful.   הִנָּךְ יָפָה.

Your eyes are doves."   עֵינַיִךְ יוֹנִים."

"Behold you are beautiful, my beloved,   "הִנְּךָ יָפֶה, דוֹדִי,

    Truly handsome!   אַף נָעִים!

Truly our bed is luxuriant."   אַף־עַרְשֵׂנוּ רַעֲנָנָה."

[Shir 1:15–16]

Although it is difficult to show in an English translation, it is quite clear in the Hebrew when the man is speaking, and when the woman. This is because of the masculine and feminine prefixes and suffixes on words in Hebrew, which we do not have in English, and the difference in Hebrew between the masculine and the feminine way of saying "you."

"I am a rose of Sharon [a region in Israel],   "אֲנִי חֲבַצֶּלֶת הַשָּׁרוֹן,

    a lily of the valleys."   שׁוֹשַׁנַּת הָעֲמָקִים."

"Like a lily among thorns,   "כְּשׁוֹשַׁנָּה בֵּין הַחוֹחִים,

    thus is my beloved among women."   כֵּן רַעְיָתִי בֵּין הַבָּנוֹת."

[Shir 2:1–2]

118

"The voice of my beloved! | ‏"קוֹל דּוֹדִי,‏

Behold, he is coming, | ‏הִנֵּה־זֶה בָּא,‏

leaping over the mountains, | ‏מְדַלֵּג עַל־הֶהָרִים,‏

skipping over the hills!" | ‏מְקַפֵּץ עַל־הַגְּבָעוֹת."‏

[Shir 2:8]

The words of Shir Hashirim have been the inspiration of countless songs, both in liturgical use and in popular music. Quotations from this book sound like a list of the Israeli hit parade. You may recognize the following lines as a song that has become popular in recent years both among youth groups and in creative temple services:

My beloved answers and says to me: | ‏עָנָה דוֹדִי וְאָמַר לִי:‏

"Get yourself up, my beloved! | ‏"קוּמִי לָךְ רַעְיָתִי!‏

My beautiful one, get yourself going! | ‏יָפָתִי וּלְכִי־לָךְ!‏

For behold, the winter has passed, | ‏כִּי הִנֵּה הַסְּתָו עָבָר,‏

the rain has gone away." | ‏הַגֶּשֶׁם חָלַף הָלַךְ לוֹ:"‏

[Shir 2:10–11]

PRAYER VOCABULARY

my beloved	דּוֹדִי	my beautiful one	יָפָתִי
the mountains	הֶהָרִים	the winter	הַסְּתָו
get yourself up	קוּמִי	the rain	הַגֶּשֶׁם
my beloved	רַעְיָתִי		

Focus on Linguistic Change

Languages change over the course of time. Just think about how strange the language of Shakespeare, who lived about five hundred years ago, sounds to us. Among other things, such as grammar, syntax, and pronunciation, words sometimes also change their meaning over the years. Hebrew has been around for close to three thousand years! In that time, remarkably little has changed, relatively speaking. However, even Israelis often have to refer to a dictionary in order to understand what is written in the Bible. An example of a word that has changed meaning since the time of the Bible is the word סְתָו. From the context of Shir Hashirim 2:11, it is clear that סְתָו was the time of year when the rain fell. In Israel, that is the winter. The ancient Jew did not think in terms of four seasons. There was the rainy winter, the spring, when the crops were planted, and the summer, when the crops were harvested. But when Eliezer Ben-Yehudah, the "father" of modern Hebrew, set out to modernize the Hebrew language, he needed a word for the season between summer and winter, which we call the fall or autumn, and the word that he chose was סְתָו. And that is what the word means in Israel today.

The following two verses are popular quotations used to decorate the Ketubah, the Jewish marriage contract. Why do you think this is so?

"My beloved is mine, and I am his.   "דוֹדִי לִי וַאֲנִי לוֹ.

He is a shepherd among the lilies."   הָרֹעֶה בַּשּׁוֹשַׁנִּים."

[Shir 2:16]

"I have found the one that my soul loves."   "מָצָאתִי אֵת שֶׁאָהֲבָה נַפְשִׁי."

[Shir 3:4b]

Near the end of the book, the author of Shir Hashirim comes to some conclusions regarding the nature and the power of love.

"Put me like a seal upon your heart,	שִׂימֵנִי כַחוֹתָם עַל-לִבֶּךָ, "
like a seal upon your arm.	כַּחוֹתָם עַל-זְרוֹעֶךָ.
For love is as strong as death,	כִּי-עַזָּה כַמָּוֶת אַהֲבָה,
jealousy is more enduring than Sheol [the afterworld].	קָשָׁה כִשְׁאוֹל קִנְאָה.
Its arrows are arrows of fire,	רְשָׁפֶיהָ רִשְׁפֵּי אֵשׁ,
a burning flame.	שַׁלְהֶבֶתְיָה.
Mighty waters are unable	מַיִם רַבִּים לֹא יוּכְלוּ
to quench love,	לְכַבּוֹת אֶת-הָאַהֲבָה,
and rivers cannot drown it."	וּנְהָרוֹת לֹא יִשְׁטְפוּהָ. "

[Shir 8:6–7a]

After reading passages like this, it is difficult not to sense the power of love; whether it is between man and woman, or a people and God. Shir Hashirim can represent for us an ideal existence toward which we can strive. Its strong emotion, combined with its emphasis on enduring love, show that there is a spark of the Divine in the mysterious relationship between a man and a woman, which we call love. And that this physical relationship is very much a part of life.

PRAYER VOCABULARY

the shepherd	הָרֹעֶה	your heart	לִבֶּךָ
among the lilies	בַּשׁוֹשַׁנִּים	your arm	זְרוֹעֶךָ
like a seal	כַחוֹתָם	fire	אֵשׁ
		and rivers	וּנְהָרוֹת

121

סְפִירַת הָעֹמֶר
COUNTING THE OMER: FROM PESACH UNTIL SHAVUOT

As we have seen, many Jewish holidays are based on the annual agricultural cycle. Passover was the time of the early spring harvest, Shavuot the time of the summer harvest. The days between Passover and Shavuot were very important for farmers. Farmers would ask God for good crops in the coming season. Biblical law did not allow farmers to eat their grain until a portion of it had been offered at the Temple. The amount of grain set aside was measured as an *omer*. According to the Bible, this *omer* of grain was offered on the second day of Passover. When offering the grain, the priest would ask God to protect the crops that would grow during the following weeks from the harsh winds.

Not only farmers were aware of a special time between Passover and Shavuot. In the Bible, God commanded all of Israel to count the days and weeks between these two holidays. This counting is known as *Sefirat Ha'Omer* (the Counting of the Omer). Every day for forty-nine days, starting on the second day of Passover, Jews traditionally count the Omer. The blessing for the counting is the same every day, only the number changes daily:

Blessed are you, Adonai our God,

 Ruler of the universe,

 who has sanctified us with his mitzvot

 and commanded us to count the Omer.

בָּרוּךְ אַתָּה יְהֹוָה

אֱלֹהֵינוּ מֶלֶךְ הָעוֹלָם,

אֲשֶׁר קִדְּשָׁנוּ בְּמִצְוֹתָיו,

וְצִוָּנוּ עַל סְפִירַת הָעֹמֶר:

Then the formula for the counting is recited:

Today is ——— of the Omer.

הַיּוֹם, יוֹם ——— בָּעֹמֶר.

The blank space is filled in differently every day:

One day.

יוֹם אֶחָד,

Two days.

שְׁנֵי יָמִים,

Seven days,

הַיּוֹם, שִׁבְעָה יָמִים,

 which was the week of the Omer.

שֶׁהֵם שָׁבוּעַ אֶחָד בָּעֹמֶר.

The counting finally ends on the day before Shavuot:

Today is the forty-ninth day,

הַיּוֹם תִּשְׁעָה וְאַרְבָּעִים יוֹם,

 which is seven weeks of the Omer.

שֶׁהֵם שִׁבְעָה שָׁבוּעוֹת, בָּעֹמֶר.

PRAYER VOCABULARY	
counting of the Omer	סְפִירַת הָעֹמֶר
today	הַיּוֹם
one week	שָׁבוּעַ
weeks	שָׁבוּעוֹת

A PERIOD OF MOURNING

The days between Passover and Shavuot are considered a solemn time. In ancient Israel the farmers would be waiting to see if the harvest would be a good one. At a later time in history, this solemn period took on the air of mourning. According to a tradition, this is the time of year when a plague took the lives of many of Rabbi Akiva's students. Because the days of the Omer are very sad, many customs of mourning prevail. Traditional Jews won't cut their hair during this time. Celebrations are forbidden, and so marriages do not take place during the counting of the Omer. There is, however, one exception to this. A joyous celebration is held on the thirty-third day of the Omer.

Focus on Another Reason for Counting the Omer

After the Temple was destroyed, Jews were scattered throughout the Diaspora, and few remained farmers. Counting the Omer lost much of its significance. Since the Bible said that it was a mitzvah (commandment) to count the Omer, the rabbinical leaders of the Jewish community had to find another reason for continuing this tradition. One such reason is given in a Midrash which ties in the significance of Passover (the Exodus) and Shavuot (the giving of the Torah) with the Omer. According to this Midrash, while the Israelites were still slaves in Egypt, they were told that fifty days after the Exodus they would receive the Torah. The Israelites were so excited that once the Exodus took place they began to count the days until the Torah would be given to them. Every day that they counted, the Israelites said, "Today we have to wait one less day for the Torah." To remember the counting done by the Israelites awaiting the Torah, there is a commandment in the Bible to count the days between Pesach and Shavuot.

לַג בָּעֹמֶר
LAG BA'OMER

Lag Ba'Omer, the thirty-third day of the counting of the Omer, is a holiday celebrated with picnics and bonfires. It commemorates a few events that are believed to have taken place on this day. The great Rabbi Akiva, although he had only learned how to read and write as an adult, was famous throughout Israel for his wisdom. Many students came to study with him. At one time, a plague struck, killing a number of Rabbi Akiva's students. The plague ended on Lag Ba'Omer, making this a joyous occasion.

Some think that Lag Ba'Omer is connected with Roman persecution. During the time of Rabbi Akiva, the Roman rulers decreed that no Jew could study Torah. Not only did Rabbi Akiva and his students disobey this decree, but Rabbi Akiva's students fought against the Roman soldiers. On Lag Ba'Omer, the Jews celebrated a victory against the Romans. That is why it is a custom among Israeli children to play with homemade bows and arrows on this holiday.

One final reason for celebrating Lag Ba'Omer concerns a student of Rabbi Akiva's named Rabbi Shimon Bar Yochai. He too taught the Torah despite the Roman ban. When the Romans found out, Rabbi Shimon Bar Yochai had to flee. He hid in a cave on Mount Meron, which is in the upper Galilee, near Safed (also known as Tsefat, which later became a center of mystical study—see p 117). His students would come to study in the cave. The students fooled the Roman soldiers by taking bows and arrows and pretending they were going hunting. This is another reason children play with bows and arrows on Lag Ba'Omer. Rabbi Shimon Bar Yochai is said to have died on Lag Ba'Omer.

What all these stories show is that the holiday of Lag Ba'Omer is a celebration of learning. It is a tribute to all Jews who managed to study Jewish traditions and Torah despite persecution.

פִּרְקֵי אָבוֹת
PIRKE AVOT

On Lag Ba'Omer we take time out from mourning the hardships suffered by ancient Jewish scholars in order to celebrate their accomplishments. During the rest of the counting of the Omer, from Passover to Shavuot, it is traditional to spend each Shabbat in studying the words of great Jewish sages.

Their wisdom is found in a book called *Pirke Avot* (the Chapters of the Fathers). This is actually a section in the collection known as the Mishnah. While the Torah is called the written law (*torah she-bichtav*), the Mishnah is referred to as the oral law (*torah she-be'al peh*). It contains basic Jewish laws divided into different categories. It is said to cover Jewish tradition, transmitted orally, from the time of the giving of the Torah. The Mishnah in its final form dates to about the year 200 C.E.

Pirke Avot contains the teachings of about sixty rabbis who lived during a five-hundred-year-period, from 300 B.C.E. to 200 C.E. In Pirke Avot, we find their beliefs on how people should behave toward each other and toward God. Pirke Avot begins by stating the credentials of these teachers, showing that their traditions go back to the giving of the Torah:

THE INTRODUCTION

Moses received the Torah at Sinai	מֹשֶׁה קִבֵּל תּוֹרָה מִסִּינַי.
and gave it to Joshua,	וּמְסָרָהּ לִיהוֹשֻׁעַ,
Joshua to the elders,	וִיהוֹשֻׁעַ לִזְקֵנִים,
and the elders to the prophets,	וּזְקֵנִים לִנְבִיאִים,
and the prophets gave it	וּנְבִיאִים מְסָרוּהָ
to the men of the Great Assembly.	לְאַנְשֵׁי כְּנֶסֶת הַגְּדוֹלָה.

[Avot 1:1]

127

The "men of the Great Assembly" is usually taken to mean the rabbis of the early Second Temple period. In the first few chapters, they are each listed by name, followed by a statement each made about living a proper life:

ON WHAT THE WORLD DEPENDS

Shimon the Just was one of the	שִׁמְעוֹן הַצַּדִּיק,
last survivors of the Great Assembly.	הָיָה מִשְׁיָרֵי כְּנֶסֶת הַגְּדוֹלָה.
He used to say:	הוּא הָיָה אוֹמֵר,
"The world depends on three things—	"עַל־שְׁלשָׁה דְבָרִים הָעוֹלָם עוֹמֵד,
on Torah, on divine service,	עַל הַתּוֹרָה, וְעַל הָעֲבוֹדָה,
and on charitable deeds."	וְעַל גְּמִילוּת חֲסָדִים."

[Avot 1:2]

The rabbis also gave advice about how to behave toward others.

Yose ben Yochanan, of Jerusalem, says:	יוֹסֵי בֶּן־יוֹחָנָן, אִישׁ יְרוּשָׁלַיִם, אוֹמֵר:
"Let your house be open wide	"יְהִי בֵיתְךָ, פָּתוּחַ לָרְוָחָה
and let the poor be	וְיִהְיוּ עֲנִיִּים
members of your household."	בְּנֵי בֵיתֶךָ."

[Avot 1:5]

PRAYER VOCABULARY			
received	קִבֵּל	the divine service	הָעֲבוֹדָה
and gave it	וּמְסָרָהּ	charitable deeds	גְּמִילוּת חֲסָדִים
to the elders	לִזְקֵנִים	open wide	פָּתוּחַ לָרְוָחָה
to the prophets	לִנְבִיאִים	members of your household	בְּנֵי בֵיתֶךָ
Great Assembly	כְּנֶסֶת הַגְּדוֹלָה		

They also made statements concerning the status and responsibilities of the individual person. One of the most famous statements was made by Hillel:

If I am not for myself,	אִם אֵין אֲנִי לִי,
who will be for me?	מִי לִי?
If I am only for myself,	וּכְשֶׁאֲנִי לְעַצְמִי,
what am I?	מָה אָנִי?
And if not now,	וְאִם לֹא עַכְשָׁו,
when?	אֵימָתָי?

[Avot 1:14]

This statement is a shorthand way of saying that a person has to watch out for his or her own good, but must take care not to be concerned just with him or herself. What do you think is meant by "And if not now, when"?

PRAYER VOCABULARY

for myself	לְעַצְמִי
now	עַכְשָׁו
when	אֵימָתַי

The rabbis gave advice on drinking (not too much), talking (make sure there is substance in it), companions (stay away from bad company), and government (power corrupts). Many of their sayings take the form of placing people in categories. They hoped to teach correct behavior by doing this.

Ben Zoma said: בֶּן־זוֹמָא אוֹמֵר:

"Who is wise? "אֵיזֶהוּ חָכָם,

The one who learns from every person. הַלּוֹמֵד מִכָּל־אָדָם.

Who is strong? אֵיזֶהוּ גִבּוֹר?

The one who controls his desires. הַכּוֹבֵשׁ אֶת־יִצְרוֹ.

Who is rich? אֵיזֶהוּ עָשִׁיר?

The one who is happy with what he has. הַשָּׂמֵחַ בְּחֶלְקוֹ.

Who is honored? אֵיזֶהוּ מְכֻבָּד?

The one who respects all creatures." הַמְכַבֵּד אֶת־הַבְּרִיּוֹת. "

[Avot 4:1]

PRAYER VOCABULARY

wise	חָכָם
strong	גִבּוֹר
his desires	יִצְרוֹ
who is happy	הַשָּׂמֵחַ
is honored	מְכֻבָּד
creatures	בְּרִיּוֹת

The power of the universal truths of the many observations made by the rabbis in Pirke Avot has not diminished with the passing of time. This is one reason their sayings are still popular today.

Jews read Pirke Avot between Passover and Shavuot. This combines the oral Jewish tradition with the written tradition, the Torah, which was received on Shavuot. Some Ashkenazi Jews continue reading Pirke Avot throughout the long Sabbath days of the summer months. This is why many traditional Siddurim contain all of Pirke Avot.

Selections from Pirke Avot can also be found in modern Siddurim. A number of selections from Pirke Avot are used as supplementary readings in the Conservative Siddur. There is also a section of sayings from Pirke Avot at the beginning of *Gates of Prayer*.

The hopes of the authors of Pirke Avot are still very much the hopes of Jews today. Pirke Avot was meant to be a guide leading to a good life. The ideas presented in it can be summarized by one saying from this collection. Though the thought is over a thousand years old, it is still quite modern:

ON WHAT THE WORLD DEPENDS—ANOTHER VIEW

Rabban Shimon ben Gamliel says: רַבָּן שִׁמְעוֹן בֶּן־גַּמְלִיאֵל אוֹמֵר:

"The world is kept alive by three things— עַל שְׁלֹשָׁה דְבָרִים הָעוֹלָם עוֹמֵד,

by truth, by justice, and by peace." עַל־הָאֱמֶת, וְעַל־הַדִּין, וְעַל הַשָּׁלוֹם."

[Avot 1:18]

PRAYER VOCABULARY

the truth	הָאֱמֶת
the justice	הַדִּין
the peace	הַשָּׁלוֹם

שָׁבוּעוֹת
SHAVUOT:
THE GIVING OF THE TORAH

The Torah readings for Pesach brought the Israelites out of Egypt, and out of the range of the Egyptian armies. The Torah reading for Shavuot tells us about what happened seven weeks (*shavuot*) after the Exodus, namely, the giving of the Torah.

When we say "Torah," we can mean a number of things. The first thing that probably comes to mind is the collection of five books that we read from in the synagogue. These first five books of the Bible, also known as the Five Books of Moses, are the foundation of the Jewish religion. However, the word *Torah* itself means "teaching" or "instruction." It can refer to the whole body of Jewish teaching. Many Jews refer to both a written and an oral Torah. What the written Torah is, is obvious. The oral Torah refers to the body of teaching that was handed down orally until it was codified in the Mishnah and the Gemara, which together make up the Talmud. Traditional Judaism would say that the whole body of Jewish teaching, both the written and the oral Torah, was given at Mount Sinai on Shavuot. The Bible only talks about what we call the Ten Commandments, and the laws that follow them.

AT SINAI

Once the Israelites had left Egypt, they wandered in the Sinai Peninsula until they came to Mount Sinai. It was there that God was to establish his covenant with the whole people, and not just with individuals, as he had during the patriarchal and matriarchal period.

132

GOD SPEAKS

Moses went up to God,

   and Adonai called to him from the

      mountain:

"Thus you shall speak to the house of Jacob

   and say to the house of Israel:

וּמֹשֶׁה עָלָה אֶל־הָאֱלֹהִים,

וַיִּקְרָא אֵלָיו יְהוָֹה

מִן־הָהָר לֵאמֹר:

״כֹּה תֹאמַר לְבֵית יַעֲקֹב

וְתַגֵּיד לִבְנֵי יִשְׂרָאֵל:

THE PAST

'You saw what I did to Egypt,

   when I lifted you on eagles' wings

   and brought you to me.

אַתֶּם רְאִיתֶם אֲשֶׁר עָשִׂיתִי לְמִצְרָיִם

וָאֶשָּׂא אֶתְכֶם עַל־כַּנְפֵי נְשָׁרִים

וָאָבִא אֶתְכֶם אֵלָי.

THE PROMISE

Now, if you will listen to my voice

   and keep my covenant,

     you will be my treasured possession

      among all the peoples.

For all the earth is mine.

But you will be

   a kingdom of priests for me,

   and a holy nation.'

These are the words which you shall say to

   the Israelites."

וְעַתָּה אִם־שָׁמוֹעַ תִּשְׁמְעוּ בְּקֹלִי

וּשְׁמַרְתֶּם אֶת־בְּרִיתִי

וִהְיִיתֶם לִי סְגֻלָּה

מִכָּל־הָעַמִּים.

כִּי לִי כָּל־הָאָרֶץ.

וְאַתֶּם תִּהְיוּ־לִי

מַמְלֶכֶת כֹּהֲנִים,

וְגוֹי קָדוֹשׁ,

אֵלֶּה הַדְּבָרִים

אֲשֶׁר תְּדַבֵּר אֶל־בְּנֵי יִשְׂרָאֵל.״

[Ex 19:3–6]

Moses then presented God's proposition to the people.

THE PEOPLE ANSWER

All the people answered as one	וַיַּעֲנוּ כָל־ הָעָם יַחְדָּו.
and said,	וַיֹּאמְרוּ,
"We will do everything that Adonai	"כֹּל אֲשֶׁר־דִּבֶּר יְהוָה
commands!"	נַעֲשֶׂה!"
So Moses conveyed the people's words	וַיָּשֶׁב מֹשֶׁה אֶת־דִּבְרֵי
back to Adonai.	הָעָם אֶל־יְיָ.

[Ex 19:8]

The stage was set for the making of the covenant between God and the Israelites. God announced that he would appear to the people on the third day at Mount Sinai. In the interim, the people were to prepare by making themselves holy. Finally,

PRAYER VOCABULARY

eagles' wings	כַּנְפֵי נְשָׁרִים	treasured possession	סְגֻלָּה
to my voice	בְּקֹלִי	kingdom of priests	מַמְלֶכֶת כֹּהֲנִים
my covenant	בְּרִיתִי		

134

GOD APPEARS

On the third day, at daybreak,	וַיְהִי בַיּוֹם הַשְּׁלִישִׁי בִּהְיֹת הַבֹּקֶר,
there was thunder, and lightning,	וַיְהִי קֹלֹת, וּבְרָקִים,
and a heavy cloud over the mountain,	וְעָנָן כָּבֵד עַל־הָהָר
and a very loud shofar blast.	וְקֹל שֹׁפָר חָזָק מְאֹד.
And all the people in the camp trembled..	וַיֶּחֱרַד כָּל־הָעָם אֲשֶׁר בַּמַּחֲנֶה.
Then Moses brought the people	וַיּוֹצֵא מֹשֶׁה אֶת־הָעָם
out of the camp to encounter God,	לִקְרַאת הָאֱלֹהִים מִן־הַמַּחֲנֶה,
and they stationed themselves at the foot	וַיִּתְיַצְּבוּ בְּתַחְתִּית
of the mountain.	הָהָר.
All of Mount Sinai was enveloped in smoke,	וְהַר סִינַי עָשַׁן כֻּלּוֹ,
since Adonai had descended upon it	מִפְּנֵי אֲשֶׁר יָרַד עָלָיו
aflame.	יְהֹוָה בָּאֵשׁ.
Its smoke went up	וַיַּעַל עֲשָׁנוֹ
like the smoke from a furnace,	כְּעֶשֶׁן הַכִּבְשָׁן,
and all of the mountain trembled	וַיֶּחֱרַד כָּל־הָהָר מְאֹד.
furiously.	

[Ex 19:16–18]

Because of the holiness of the moment, only Moses, Aaron, and the priests were allowed to come any closer. And then, in this awe-inspiring setting, God spoke the words which we now call the Ten Commandments, which have formed the basis of the Jewish religion and its code of ethics down to this very day.

PRAYER VOCABULARY			
thunder	קֹלֹת	in the camp	בַּמַּחֲנֶה
and lightening	וּבְרָקִים	and they stationed themselves	וַיִּתְיַצְּבוּ
and a cloud	וְעָנָן	all of the mountain	כָּל־הָהָר

שָׁבוּעוֹת
SHAVUOT:
THE BOOK OF RUTH

The *Book of Ruth* is the second of the Five Megillot, coming after Shir Hashirim, which is read on Pesach, and before Eicha, which is read on Tisha B'Av. It is read during Shavuot because most of the action of the book takes place during the barley and wheat harvests of early to mid-summer. Shavuot is the holiday of the first harvest, and it also celebrates the giving of the Torah. Other reasons given in traditional literature for Ruth's being read at this time include the theme of Ruth's conversion to Judaism and acceptance of the Torah, and the connection to King David, who is supposed to have died at this time of year.

More than anything else, the Book of Ruth is a great short story. Love, devotion, and faith are its major themes. In masterful style it tells the story of Naomi and her daughter-in-law Ruth, both widowed and alone in the world. From this bleak beginning a suspenseful tale is woven that leads to a happy ending not only for both of them, but also for the Jewish people, since King David was to be Ruth's grandson.

Many great stories start off with "Once upon a time," and the story of
Ruth, using a Hebrew equivalent, of course, is no exception.

Once, during the days   וַיְהִי בִּימֵי

when the judges judged,   שְׁפֹט הַשֹּׁפְטִים,

there was a famine in the land.   וַיְהִי רָעָב בָּאָרֶץ

So, a man from Bethlehem in Judah   וַיֵּלֶךְ אִישׁ מִבֵּית לֶחֶם יְהוּדָה

went to live in the steppes of Moab,   לָגוּר בִּשְׂדֵי מוֹאָב,

he, and his wife, and his two sons.   הוּא וְאִשְׁתּוֹ וּשְׁנֵי בָנָיו.

The name of the man was Elimelech,   וְשֵׁם הָאִישׁ אֱלִימֶלֶךְ,

and the name of his wife was Naomi,   וְשֵׁם אִשְׁתּוֹ נָעֳמִי,

and the names of his two sons were   וְשֵׁם שְׁנֵי־בָנָיו

Machlon and Kilion.   [Ruth 1:1–2]   מַחְלוֹן וְכִלְיוֹן.

Once in Moab, Elimelech died, leaving Naomi with her two
sons, who married Moabite women, Orpah and Ruth. However,
after about ten years, Machlon and Kilion also died, leaving the
three women alone.

Focus on Hebrew Names

Since the time of the Bible, Hebrew names have been chosen
because of their meaning. So too in the Book of Ruth. Elimelech, like
most biblical names, contains the word "God." The name means
"God is my king." Naomi means "the pleasant one." Later on in the
story, when she is sad and alone, she makes a pun on her name and
says, "Don't call me Naomi, 'the pleasant one,' call me Marah, 'the
bitter one' " (Ruth 1:20). The two boys, Machlon and Kilion, who died
at a young age, were named "the sick one" and "the short-lived one."
No one is really sure what the name Ruth means. The Midrash says
that she was named Ruth because she "saw" (*ra'athah*) what Naomi
told her (about Judaism).

PRAYER VOCABULARY

judges	שֹׁפְטִים	his wife	אִשְׁתּוֹ
famine	רָעָב		

137

At this time, Naomi heard that God had ended the famine in Judah, so she set out to return to her hometown of Bethlehem. Orpah and Ruth didn't want her to go alone, so they set out with her. Naomi managed to convince Orpah to return to her home in Moab. But Ruth refused to desert her mother-in-law and decided to join her fate to Naomi's:

But Ruth said:	וַתֹּאמֶר רוּת:
"Don't force me to leave you,	אַל־תִּפְגְּעִי־בִי לְעָזְבֵךְ
to return from following after you.	לָשׁוּב מֵאַחֲרָיִךְ
For wherever you go, I will go.	כִּי אֶל־אֲשֶׁר תֵּלְכִי אֵלֵךְ.
And wherever you stay, I will stay.	וּבַאֲשֶׁר תָּלִינִי אָלִין.
Your people are my people.	עַמֵּךְ עַמִּי.
And your God is my God.	וֵאלֹהַיִךְ אֱלֹהָי.
Wherever you die, I will die;	בַּאֲשֶׁר תָּמוּתִי אָמוּת;
and there will I be buried.	וְשָׁם אֶקָּבֵר.
Thus may the Lord do to me, and more,	כֹּה יַעֲשֶׂה יְהוָה לִי וְכֹה יֹסִיף,
if even death shall come	כִּי הַמָּוֶת יַפְרִיד
between me and you."	בֵּינִי וּבֵינֵךְ.

[Ruth 1:16–17]

With these inspired words, Ruth has become the model for all future converts to Judaism.

PRAYER VOCABULARY

to leave you	לְעָזְבֵךְ	and, your God	וֵאלֹהַיִךְ
wherever you stay	בַּאֲשֶׁר תָּלִינִי	is my God	אֱלֹהָי
I will stay	אָלִין	shall come between	יַפְרִיד

Focus on Naomi's Half of the Conversation

The rabbis who wrote the Midrash to Ruth viewed the lines quoted above as answers Ruth gave to Naomi. According to their interpretation, when Ruth decided to stay with Naomi, she showed her willingness to be converted. Naomi tried to convince her not to convert because she would be accepting many hardships, but Ruth had an answer to everything that Naomi said.

Naomi: You won't be able to attend theaters and circuses.*

Ruth: Wherever you go, I will go.

Naomi: You will have to live in a house which has a mezuzah on the door.

Ruth: Wherever you stay, I will stay.

Naomi: Jews are forbidden to do many things.

Ruth: Your people are my people.

Naomi: There are many commandments that Jews must follow.

Ruth: Your God is my God.

In her last two responses, the rabbis believed that Ruth accepted the Jewish people and their religion.

These ancient forms of entertainment were frowned upon because they were considered to appeal to the worst in human nature.

Once in Bethlehem, Naomi and Ruth lived a simple life, with Ruth caring for their needs by going into the fields and collecting grain after the harvesters. However, the field that Ruth happened to be gleaning in belonged to Boaz, a distant relative of Naomi's. Boaz was impressed with the young Moabite woman and instructed his workers to take special care of her. Then, slowly but surely, Boaz and Ruth began to fall in love. However, one more obstacle would have to be overcome before the story could end happily.

THE LEVIRATE - YIBBUM

In ancient times there was a law known as the Law of Levirate Marriage, or in Hebrew יִבּוּם. It said that if a married man died childless, his nearest relative would have to marry his widow so that the first child born of such a union could inherit the dead man's property. Ruth's dead husband, Machlon, had one relative closer than Boaz. He had to be given the first chance to marry Ruth. However, he was worried about the legal problems associated with such a marriage. What would happen with his own inheritance and any other children that he might have? Therefore he relinquished his claim on Ruth, freeing Boaz, the second in line, and Ruth to get married to each other.

It is ironic to note that the relative who was so concerned with his own inheritance and its loss if he should marry Ruth is completely forgotten in Jewish tradition. The Bible just refers to him as פְּלוֹנִי אַלְמוֹנִי, which means something like "good old what's-his-name."

The story ends with the rejoicing over the birth of Ruth and Boaz's son Oved, the father of Jesse, the father of David. Thus a convert became the grandmother of the greatest Jewish hero, and a "mother of royalty."

These are the generations of Peretz:	וְאֵלֶּה תּוֹלְדוֹת פָּרֶץ:
Peretz was the father of Hetzron.	פֶּרֶץ הוֹלִיד אֶת־חֶצְרוֹן.
And Hetzron was the father of Ram.	וְחֶצְרוֹן הוֹלִיד אֶת־רָם.
And Ram was the father of Amminadav.	וְרָם הוֹלִיד אֶת־עַמִּינָדָב.
And Amminadav was the father of Nachshon.	וְעַמִּינָדָב הוֹלִיד אֶת־נַחְשׁוֹן.
And Nachshon was the father of Salmah.	וְנַחְשׁוֹן הוֹלִיד אֶת־שַׂלְמָה.
And Salmon was the father of Boaz.	וְשַׂלְמוֹן הוֹלִיד אֶת־בֹּעַז.
And Boaz was the father of Oved.	וּבֹעַז הוֹלִיד אֶת־עוֹבֵד.
And Oved was the father of Jesse.	וְעֹבֵד הוֹלִיד אֶת־יִשָׁי.
And Jesse was the father of David.	וְיִשַׁי הוֹלִיד אֶת־דָּוִד.

[Ruth 4:18–22]

PRAYER VOCABULARY

generations	תּוֹלְדוֹת
was the father of	הוֹלִיד

141

What makes the Book of Ruth so special? First, it is a very moving story about good people and how they overcame adversity through faith, love, and hard work.

Second, the Book of Ruth is an eloquent plea for the acceptance of converts into the Jewish community. By highlighting the goodness of Ruth, who was born a Moabite, and showing her whole-hearted devotion to Judaism and the Jewish community, the Book of Ruth is teaching us that there is no difference between one who was born a Jew and one who has become a Jew by choice. After all, a convert was the ancestor of Kings David and Solomon and all their descendants.

And last, but certainly not least, the Book of Ruth is also one of many stories in the Bible in which a woman is the main character and actor. Other such stories include those of Eve and Adam, Deborah and Barak, Esther and Mordechai, and Tamar and Judah. In all of these stories, and more, the outcome is determined by the woman's action. However, the Book of Ruth is special even in this regard, since in it there are *two* women, Ruth *and* Naomi, without whom the happy ending would have been impossible.

AN ALL–PURPOSE PRAYER

Like the other Jewish festivals, there are special prayers associated
with the holiday of Shavuot. These prayers thank God for giving us
this holiday and for giving us the Torah. While the prayers mention
Shavuot specifically, the words of these prayers are familiar. This is
because there are a number of prayers that have the same structure,
only the specific words change in order to fit the specific holiday—be
it Pesach, Sukkot, Shemini Atzeret, Simchat Torah, or Shavuot.

One such "all-purpose" prayer can be found in the *Amidah*.
Amidah means "standing." It refers to the prayers which we read
silently in the synagogue while standing. The Amidah changes to suit
the occasion. The weekday Amidah is also called the *Shemoneh-esre*
(שְׁמוֹנֶה עֶשְׂרֵה), the "eighteen." This is a reference to the eighteen
benedictions that make up the Amidah in the traditional prayerbook.
Actually, this is inaccurate, since there are nineteen prayers in the
Amidah. The Shabbat and festival Amidah consists of seven benedictions. The Rosh Hashanah Amidah has nine blessings.

THE AMIDAH

The structure of the Amidah itself can also be seen as a sandwich. In all the Amidot throughout the year, the first and last three prayers are the same. The middle blessings, or "filling," are changed to suit the flavor of the holiday or occasion.

When a person reads the Amidah silently, the person is talking to God. In the first three prayers, one approaches God, honoring God the way one would honor a ruler. This is also why we bow at the beginning of the Amidah. In the last three prayers, one takes leave of God the way one would leave a ruler, by thanking God for his deeds. Again, one bows at the end of the Amidah. During the weekday, the middle blessings are "petitions," asking God for health, protection, and other good things. The rabbis thought that it would be inappropriate to petition God on Shabbat and holidays. This is why the middle blessings for these occasions differ from the weekday version.

KEDUSHAT HAYOM

Instead of petitioning God on Shabbat and festival days in the middle blessings, we mention the holiday, its meaning, and thank God for giving us this special day. This is called *Kedushat Hayom,* the "sanctification of the day." It is a prayer both of praise and of thanksgiving.

Focus on Jewish Prayer

When we look at the Siddur, it can be overwhelming. There are pages and pages of prayers in it. There is, however, one prayer which is considered to be the essence of the service, the Amidah. In the Talmud, the Amidah is called the *tefillah,* the "Prayer." A Jew's obligation to pray was fulfilled by reciting the Amidah. All the other parts of the prayer service are built around the Amidah. Additions to the service have been made throughout history, but the Amidah still remained the focus. It is as though the Amidah were the filling in a sandwich, which gives the whole its character.

You have chosen us from all the nations,

אַתָּה בְחַרְתָּנוּ מִכָּל־הָעַמִּים,

    You have loved us, you have favored us,

אָהַבְתָּ אוֹתָנוּ. וְרָצִיתָ בָּנוּ.

    You have exalted us

וְרוֹמַמְתָּנוּ

        above all other tongues,

מִכָּל־הַלְּשׁוֹנוֹת,

  And you have sanctified us

וְקִדַּשְׁתָּנוּ

      with your commandments.

בְּמִצְוֹתֶיךָ.

You have brought us close to you, our ruler,

וְקֵרַבְתָּנוּ מַלְכֵּנוּ

    to serve you,

לַעֲבוֹדָתֶךָ,

  and have called us to your great and holy

וְשִׁמְךָ הַגָּדוֹל וְהַקָּדוֹשׁ

    name.

עָלֵינוּ קָרָאתָ.

What makes the Kedushat Hayom special is that it changes while staying the same. The basic words in it remain the same for the holidays, only the name of the specific holiday changes. This is the Kedushat Hayom for Shavuot.

PRAYER VOCABULARY

you have chosen us	בְּחַרְתָּנוּ
you have loved us	אָהַבְתָּ אוֹתָנוּ
you have favored us	רָצִיתָ בָּנוּ
you have exalted us	רוֹמַמְתָּנוּ
you have sanctified us	קִדַּשְׁתָּנוּ
you have brought us close to you	קֵרַבְתָּנוּ

With love you have given us, Adonai our God,	וַתִּתֶּן לָנוּ יְהֹוָה אֱלֹהֵינוּ בְּאַהֲבָה,
(Sabbaths for rest and) holidays for joy,	[שַׁבָּתוֹת וּ]מוֹעֲדִים לְשִׂמְחָה,
festivals and seasons for rejoicing:	חַגִּים וּזְמַנִּים לְשָׂשׂוֹן:
(this Sabbath day and)	אֶת־יוֹם [הַשַּׁבָּת הַזֶּה וְאֶת־יוֹם]
this feast of Shavuot,	חַג הַשָּׁבֻעוֹת הַזֶּה,
the season of the giving of the Torah,	זְמַן מַתַּן תּוֹרָתֵנוּ,
(with love) a holy occasion,	[בְּאַהֲבָה] מִקְרָא קֹדֶשׁ,
commemorating the Exodus from Egypt.	זֵכֶר לִיצִיאַת מִצְרָיִם.

It is this last portion which varies. There are special phrases for Pesach, Sukkot, and Simchat Torah and Shemini Atzeret.

PRAYER VOCABULARY

the giving of the Torah	מַתַּן תּוֹרָתֵנוּ
a holy occasion	מִקְרָא קֹדֶשׁ
the Exodus from Egypt	יְצִיאַת מִצְרַיִם

The Kedushat Hayom is immediately followed by another prayer called *Ya'aleh Ve'yavo* (יַעֲלֶה וְיָבֹא). This can loosely be translated as meaning "to climb up and approach." One interpretation of this prayer is that it symbolizes the sacrifices pilgrims brought to the Temple on the pilgrimage holidays of Sukkot, Pesach, and Shavuot. In order to sacrifice one would have to climb (*ya'aleh*—יַעֲלֶה) the Temple steps and enter (*yavo*—יָבֹא) the Temple. As with the Kedushat Hayom, the name of each holiday is said in the Ya'aleh Ve'yavo at the appropriate time. Ya'aleh Ve'yavo ends with a request for the holiday:

[This day] remember us, Adonai our God, for good.	זָכְרֵנוּ יְהֹוָה אֱלֹהֵינוּ בּוֹ לְטוֹבָה.
[This day] call on us for a blessing.	וּפָקְדֵנוּ בוֹ לִבְרָכָה.
[This day] help us to live.	וְהוֹשִׁיעֵנוּ בוֹ לְחַיִּים.

The three pilgrimage festivals mentioned in the Torah are important times. Their importance is reflected in two ways. Firstly, there are special services for these holidays. Secondly, as we have seen above, the central prayers of Judaism are tailored to fit these occasions, the holidays of Sukkot, Pesach, and Shavuot.

PRAYER VOCABULARY

to climb up	יַעֲלֶה	for good	לְטוֹבָה
to enter	יָבֹא	for a blessing	לִבְרָכָה
remember us	זָכְרֵנוּ	for life/to live	לְחַיִּים

147

TWO MODERN HOLIDAYS

All the holidays discussed in this book so far have been a part of Jewish tradition for many years. Some are mentioned in the Bible, others were established by the rabbis. The special readings for these holidays also span centuries in time and numerous countries in origin. One holiday may incorporate readings from the Bible, the Talmud, and medieval sources. In this way, Jewish holidays have developed through the course of history.

Jewish communities throughout the world have celebrated their own special holidays to commemorate events affecting their town or village. For example, there are records of dozens of "special Purims" celebrated by Jewish communities saved from disaster. Today, Jews continue to commemorate occasions of importance to the Jewish people. In the twentieth century, there have been two events that have greatly affected all Jews. These are the Holocaust and the creation of the State of Israel. As in the past, the Jewish people have responded to these events by creating new holidays and liturgy to remember these events.

What makes these two modern Jewish holidays different is that they are still young; ways of commemorating Holocaust Day and Israel Independence Day are still being formed. Rabbis are in the process of establishing liturgy they feel fits these holidays. Many congregations are also taking part in this creative act. There is no set pattern, and every temple and synagogue chooses what it feels is appropriate to the holiday in question.

PRAYER VOCABULARY

Israel Independence Day	יוֹם הָעַצְמָאוּת
Holocaust Memorial Day	יוֹם הַשּׁוֹאָה

יוֹם הַשּׁוֹאָה
YOM HASHOAH: HOLOCAUST MEMORIAL DAY

During World War II one-third of the world Jewish population was murdered by the Nazis. There are few Jews in America today who do not know of some relative or relatives who were killed during this war. The destruction of six million Jews in Europe is called *Hashoah*, the Holocaust. As mentioned above, *Holocaust* is a Greek term meaning a burnt offering. When used for this modern Jewish tragedy it brings to mind the gas chambers, crematoria, and other horrors that took so many Jewish lives.

Yom Hashoah was first declared a day of remembrance by the Knesset, the Israeli parliament. In April of 1951, the Knesset passed a resolution proclaiming that Holocaust Day would be commemorated on the twenty-seventh of Nissan. This date was decided upon because it falls in the period of mourning during the counting of the Omer. The day is also halfway between the first day of Pesach, which was the day of the Warsaw Ghetto uprising, and Israel Independence Day.

For a while, in the United States, most Jews determined Holocaust Day according to the secular calendar. Yom Hashoah was commemorated on April 19th, the first day of the Warsaw Ghetto uprising according to the secular calendar.

The ways in which Jews commemorate this day vary greatly. Each congregation chooses material that it feels reflects the somber mood of this remembrance. Many synagogues and temples choose to read excerpts from items written during or about the Holocaust. These might include poems written by children in ghettos, excerpts from diaries, or descriptions of living conditions and people's attitudes toward their situation. Some suggested readings may be found in the Reform Siddur, *Gates of Prayer*.

Because Holocaust Day is a memorial day, many congregations include a special Kaddish for those who died during the Holocaust. There are many variations on this Kaddish but the style is the same. The names of ghettos and concentration camps are interspersed among the words of the Kaddish used in the daily prayer:

> Magnified and sanctified be His great name
>
> Warsaw, Lodz, Vilna
>
> In the world which He created as he saw fit
>
> Maidanek, Treblinka, Bergen-Belsen

The new Conservative *Sim Shalom* Siddur has a Kaddish in this style. Many synagogues, temples, and other Jewish organizations have created their own versions.

Another Holocaust Day variation on an old prayer is based on the *El Maleh Rachamim* ("God full of mercy"). This prayer originated in Europe and was read in memory of the victims of the Crusades. Later, it was also used for the victims of other massacres in Europe. The Chief Rabbis of Israel decided that it would be appropriate for this prayer to be used for the victims of the Holocaust. It also exists today in a number of forms:

Merciful God, grant perfect peace   אֵל מָלֵא רַחֲמִים הַמְצֵא מְנוּחָה נְכוֹנָה

under your sheltering wings,   עַל כַּנְפֵי הַשְּׁכִינָה,

among the holy and pure   בְּמַעֲלוֹת קְדוֹשִׁים וּטְהוֹרִים,

who shine as bright as the heavens,   כְּזֹוהַר הָרָקִיעַ מַזְהִירִים,

to the souls of the six million Jewish   אֶת נִשְׁמוֹתֵיהֶם שֶׁל

    martyrs   שֵׁשׁ מֵאוֹת רִבְבוֹת אַלְפֵי יִשְׂרָאֵל

who were killed, slaughtered   שֶׁנֶּהֶרְגוּ וְשֶׁנִּשְׂרְפוּ

and cremated,   וְשֶׁנִּטְבְּחוּ

    in the lands of   בְּגָלֻות

    Europe.   אֵירוֹפָּה.

May they rest in Paradise.   בְּגַן עֵדֶן תְּהֵא מְנוּחָתָם.

May the merciful One bind their souls in   בַּעַל הָרַחֲמִים יִצְרוֹר בִּצְרוֹר הַחַיִּים

    the bond of life.   אֶת נִשְׁמוֹתֵיהֶם.

Adonai is their inheritance.   יְהֹוָה הוּא נַחֲלָתָם.

He will remind us of their sacrifice.   וְיִזְכּוֹר לָנוּ עֲקֵדָתָם.

The earth will not cover up their blood,   אֶרֶץ אַל תְּכַסִּי דָמָם.

Their cries will not be silenced.   וְאַל יְהִי מָקוֹם לְזַעֲקָתָם.

May they rest in peace.   וְיָנוּחוּ עַל מִשְׁכְּבוֹתָם.

And let us say: Amen.   וְנֹאמַר אָמֵן:

PRAYER VOCABULARY

holy	קְדוֹשִׁים	in paradise	בְּגַן עֵדֶן
pure	טְהוֹרִים	their blood	דָמָם
the heavens	הָרָקִיעַ		
who were killed	שֶׁנֶּהֶרְגוּ		

יוֹם הָעַצְמָאוּת
YOM HA'ATZMAUT:
ISRAEL INDEPENDENCE DAY

The creation of the State of Israel in May of 1948 was celebrated by Jews throughout the world. The festivities for this holiday have not diminished with time. In Israel, Independence Day *(Yom Ha'atzmaut)* is celebrated on the fifth day of Iyyar. This was the day on which Israel declared its independence, according to the Jewish calendar.

Most of the festivities in Israel and the rest of the world are of a secular nature. These include parades, parties, and fireworks displays. Liturgy for this day was first determined in 1949 by Israel's Chief Rabbis. They felt that reciting psalms of thanksgiving (Psalms 97, 98, and 107) was appropriate for the day. Eventually, the Chief Rabbinate created a complete liturgical ceremony for Israel Independence Day. This includes biblical excerpts about the Land of Israel, recitation of an abridged form of the Hallel, and the blowing of the shofar.

One unusual aspect of this liturgy is that it includes a special prayer for the State of Israel. What makes this prayer unusual is that it is completely modern. Unlike the El Maleh Rachamim for Yom Hashoah, which is based on earlier prayers, the Prayer for the State of Israel has no earlier basis. While it is a twentieth-century prayer commissioned by the Chief Rabbinate, the language is in the style of earlier prayers:

Our father in heaven,	אָבִינוּ שֶׁבַשָּׁמַיִם,
rock and redeemer of Israel,	צוּר יִשְׂרָאֵל וְגוֹאֲלוֹ,
bless the State of Israel, the first blossom	בָּרֵךְ אֶת מְדִינַת יִשְׂרָאֵל,
of our deliverance.	רֵאשִׁית צְמִיחַת גְּאֻלָּתֵנוּ.
Shield it beneath your wings of	הָגֵן עָלֶיהָ בְּאֶבְרַת
righteousness,	חַסְדֶּךָ,
spread your canopy of peace over it.	וּפְרֹס עָלֶיהָ סֻכַּת שְׁלוֹמֶךָ.
Send your light and truth to its leaders,	וּשְׁלַח אוֹרְךָ וַאֲמִתְּךָ לְרָאשֶׁיהָ
officers and counselors,	שָׂרֶיהָ וְיוֹעֲצֶיהָ,
and direct them with your good counsel.	וְתַקְּנֵם בְּעֵצָה טוֹבָה מִלְּפָנֶיךָ.

The prayer then goes on to ask for strength for the defenders of the State of Israel. More importantly, this is followed by a request for peace.

Give peace in the land,	וְנָתַתָּ שָׁלוֹם בָּאָרֶץ,
and eternal joy	וְשִׂמְחַת עוֹלָם
to its inhabitants.	לְיוֹשְׁבֶיהָ.

Then there is a request for all Jews to be united in the Land of Israel. This is followed by a quotation from Deuteronomy 30:4–5 which says that God will gather the exiles from around the world. Finally there is a request to make us all better Jews and for God to make things better for all the inhabitants of the world. The prayer ends with praise of God.

PRAYER VOCABULARY

our father	אָבִינוּ	good counsel	עֵצָה טוֹבָה
rock	צוּר	eternal joy	שִׂמְחַת עוֹלָם
your light	אוֹרְךָ	to its inhabitants	לְיוֹשְׁבֶיהָ

153

Let everything that breathes say: וְיֹאמַר כֹּל אֲשֶׁר נְשָׁמָה בְּאַפּוֹ:

    Adonai, the God of Israel, is the ruler, יְיָ אֱלֹהֵי יִשְׂרָאֵל מֶלֶךְ,

    his majesty rules over everything. וּמַלְכוּתוֹ בַּכֹּל מָשָׁלָה.

    Amen. Selah. אָמֵן סֶלָה.

The Prayer for the State of Israel appears in many American Siddurim and is recited on other occasions besides Israel Independence Day. American Jews have also created their own liturgical tributes to Israel. *Gates of Prayer* includes special readings varying from biblical excerpts to modern poetry by Hannah Senesh. Conservative Siddurim contain a special *Al Hanissim* ("concerning the miracles"). This is a tribute to God said on certain holidays. There is an Al Hanissim for Purim, and a different one about the miracle associated with Chanukah. A twentieth-century version of the Al Hanissim was written thanking God for the State of Israel. As with the other Al Hanissim prayers, it too gives a short history of the holiday in question.

The religious way in which we celebrate Yom Ha'atzmaut varies from place to place. What is significant about this holiday is that American Jews want to celebrate it and are creating their own religious means of doing so. Sometimes we look to the Bible for a means of expressing our feelings. At other times, we change old prayers to fit new surroundings. We even create completely new prayers to say what we feel. All this shows that modern Jewish liturgy, as in the past, is aware of the world around it. Jews of today, like Jews throughout history, are shaping their prayers to fit their lives as Jews in a modern world.

PRAYER VOCABULARY

our father	אָבִינוּ	your light	אוֹרְךָ
heaven	שָׁמַיִם	with your good counsel	בְּעֵצָה טוֹבָה
rock	צוּר	to its inhabitants	לְיוֹשְׁבֶיהָ
shield	הַגֵּן	his majesty	מַלְכוּתוֹ

154

Focus on Who Wrote the Prayer for the State of Israel

Many Jewish prayers date far back into history. We don't know who composed a good number of them. We think we know the writers of others. When the prayer for the State of Israel first appeared, it was attributed to the Chief Rabbinate of Israel. Actually, the Chief Rabbis didn't write it. They commissioned someone else to do it. This person felt it would be better if no one knew who had written the prayer. No one did know until a few years ago, after the death of the prayer's author. The Prayer for the State of Israel was composed by Shmuel Yosef (Shai) Agnon, an Israeli writer who also won the Nobel Prize for literature. Agnon was a master at using the Hebrew language, as is evident from his use of language in the Prayer for the State of Israel.

תִּשְׁעָה בְּאָב
TISHA B'AV
A FATEFUL DAY

In the months between Shavuot and Rosh Hashanah only one major Jewish holiday is celebrated, and that is a very somber one, *Tisha B'Av*, the ninth day of the month of Av, commemorates a number of sad occasions in Jewish history, all of which traditionally took place on this very day.

First, on the ninth day of Av, according to the Talmud, both the First and the Second Temples in Jerusalem were destroyed. King Solomon, the son of David, built the First Temple in about the year 960 B.C.E. In 586 B.C.E., the Babylonians under King Nebuchadnezzar captured Jerusalem, destroyed the Temple, and exiled most of the important people to Babylon. This was the beginning of the Babylonian Exile, which you have all learned about in your religious schools. After about seventy years, some Jews were able to return to Israel, which was also called Judah, and began to rebuild the Temple. The Second Temple was finally finished in the days of Ezra and Nehemiah. Much later, King Herod the Great enlarged it and made it magnificent, one of the true wonders of the ancient world. In all, the Second Temple stood for about five hundred years. However, in the year 70 C.E., during the great Jewish revolt against Rome, Jerusalem was again destroyed on the ninth day of Av, and with it the Temple. Since then, the Jews have not had a Temple, and, until 1948, no country of their own.

156

Second, Tisha B'Av is also the day on which the second Jewish revolt against Rome ended in defeat. On that day, the revolt of Bar Kochba ended as the Romans captured the fortress of Betar in 135 C.E.

All Americans know the date 1492 as the year that "Columbus sailed the ocean blue." The discovery of America, which was to provide refuge to so many Jews over the years, was indirectly an important date in Jewish history. However, 1492 was also the year of a third type of disaster that befell the Jews on Tisha B'Av. On that day, just before Columbus set sail from Spain, the last of Spain's Jews left Spain after a century of intense persecution.

These are perhaps the most infamous disasters that have befallen the Jews on the fateful date of Tisha B'Av. The list, however, could be expanded by the addition of many more smaller, but no less tragic Tisha B'Av's in our history.

Tisha B'Av is a day of mourning. As such, many Jews fast on that day in remembrance of the awful occurrences that took place on it. In the synagogue, the *Book of Eicha* is read.

אֵיכָה
THE BOOK OF EICHA

Eicha is known by a number of names. The name Eicha is taken from the first word of the book in Hebrew, אֵיכָה ("how"). In Hebrew, the book is also called *Qinot* (קִינוֹת). This name means "lamentations," which is also the most common name of the book in English. Lamentations ("songs of mourning") is an appropriate name for the book, since it consists of five poems which mourn the destruction of Judah, Jerusalem, and the First Temple by the Babylonians. Both later Jewish and Christian tradition ascribe the writing of Eicha to the prophet Jeremiah, who lived at the time of the events that it describes. However, modern research has made that appear unlikely on the basis of stylistic and linguistic criteria. We really do not know who the author was, but we can appreciate the skill with which the poems were crafted, and the anguish that is expressed in them. They are a most fitting way to remember a day of disaster in Jewish life.

Eicha is divided up into five chapters, corresponding to the five poems that make up the book. Unlike most traditional English poetry, the poetry of the Bible does not rely very much on rhymes. The most characteristic element of biblical poetry is its structure, and the poems of Eicha are skillfully constructed.

The basis for all these poems is the Hebrew alphabet, which has twenty-two letters. Chapters 1, 2, and 4 each consist of twenty-two verses. In each chapter the verses follow the sequence of the alphabet. Thus the first word in the first verse begins with aleph, the second with bet, the third with gimel, and so on in order through all the letters. Chapter 3 is also arranged according to the alphabet, but in this case there are three verses for every letter, to make a total of sixty-six verses for this chapter. Chapter 5 is the only poem in Eicha which is not arranged according to the order of the letters of the alphabet. However, chapter 5 is made up of twenty-two verses, so that the number, if not the order, of the alphabet is still preserved. In chapters 2, 3 and 4 the order of the 'ayin and the pe is reversed. Usually 'ayin comes before pe. However, in these chapters, the pe comes before the 'ayin. No one really knows the explanation for this. It could be because the final order of the letters of the alphabet had not been completely decided on yet, and there still was confusion regarding the order of these two letters.

Eicha consists of some very vivid descriptions of the fall of Jerusalem and the depths to which that once-proud city and its inhabitants had fallen.

Focus on the Alphabet

Everyone who can read this book knows that the English alphabet has twenty-six letters. Everyone (we hope!) who has learned Hebrew knows that the Hebrew alphabet has twenty-two letters. What not so many people know is that these two alphabets are first cousins. People didn't always write using an alphabet. Before the invention of the alphabet in the ancient Near East, people used complicated systems of drawing pictures and writing in syllables. In order to read or write one had to learn hundreds, or even thousands, of different signs. The hieroglyphs of Egypt and the cuneiform writing of Mesopotamia are examples of this. However, a bit more than three thousand years ago, a revolutionary invention took place in Canaan: the alphabet was invented. Suddenly it was possible to write anything at all using less than thirty characters. Everyone else in the Near East rushed to use the alphabet for writing their language. Among others, the Hebrews started using the twenty-two letters of the Canaanite alphabet for writing Hebrew. Every culture that adopted the alphabet changed the way it was written. Eventually, the Aramaic version of writing the alphabet became the most popular, and the Jews adopted it for writing Hebrew instead of their own alphabet. Therefore, the Hebrew alphabet that we use is actually the Aramaic alphabet. Arabic is another Near Eastern (Semitic) language that uses an adaptation of the Canaanite alphabet. Meanwhile, the alphabet was also traveling westward. Phoenician traders, who were the descendants of the Canaanites, took the alphabet to Greece. There the shapes of the letters changed a bit, some new letters were added, and some old letters had different sounds associated with them. From Greece the alphabet traveled on to Rome, where the same sorts of changes took place. From Rome, the rest of Western Europe inherited the alphabet. Thus we in the English-speaking world got a version of the same alphabet that the ancient Hebrews used. English *a* = Greek alpha α = Hebrew aleph א; English *b* = Greek beta β = Hebrew bet ב; English *c* = Greek gamma γ = Hebrew gimel ג; English *d* = Greek delta δ = Hebrew dalet ד; and so on.

How she has become desolate,

    the city that was full of people!

She has become a widow,

    who was great among the nations.

The most noble among the provinces

    has become a servant.

She weeps bitterly at night,

    her tears are on her cheeks.

No one comforts her,

    from all of her lovers.

All her friends have betrayed her,

    they have become her enemies.

אֵיכָה ׀ יָשְׁבָה בָדָד,

הָעִיר רַבָּתִי עָם!

הָיְתָה כְּאַלְמָנָה,

רַבָּתִי בַגּוֹיִם.

שָׂרָתִי בַּמְּדִינוֹת

הָיְתָה לָמַס.

בָּכוֹ תִבְכֶּה בַּלַּיְלָה,

וְדִמְעָתָהּ עַל לֶחֱיָהּ.

אֵין־לָהּ מְנַחֵם,

מִכָּל־אֹהֲבֶיהָ.

כָּל־רֵעֶיהָ בָּגְדוּ בָהּ,

הָיוּ לָהּ לְאֹיְבִים.

[Lam. 1:1–2]

In this short excerpt from the first poem, one can see how Jerusalem is personified as a woman. During the course of the book she is also referred to as Zion and the daughter of Judah. Chapters 2 and 4 are also in the form of laments over the city itself. Chapter 3 is in the form of a lament by an individual eyewitness to the events, while chapter 5 is a communal lament.

PRAYER VOCABULARY

how she	אֵיכָה	on her cheeks	עַל לֶחֱיָהּ
a widow	אַלְמָנָה	her lovers	אֹהֲבֶיהָ
the city	הָעִיר	her friends	רֵעֶיהָ
among the provinces	בַּמְּדִינוֹת	enemies	אֹיְבִים
		at night	בַּלַּיְלָה

The people are left without leaders. Social order has broken down, as the loss of the law/teachings/Torah indicates. Even God seems to have abandoned Israel:

Her [Jerusalem's] gates are sunk into the earth,	טָבְעוּ בָאָרֶץ שְׁעָרֶיהָ,
He [God] has broken and destroyed her locks.	אִבַּד וְשִׁבַּר בְּרִיחֶיהָ.
Her king and nobles are among the nations [in exile],	מַלְכָּה וְשָׂרֶיהָ בַגּוֹיִם
there is no more Torah.	אֵין תּוֹרָה.
Even her prophets cannot find	גַּם־נְבִיאֶיהָ לֹא־מָצְאוּ
any more inspiration from Adonai.	חָזוֹן מֵיהוָֹה.

[Lam. 2:9]

PRAYER VOCABULARY

her [Jerusalem's] gates	שְׁעָרֶיהָ
her locks	בְּרִיחֶיהָ
her prophets	נְבִיאֶיהָ

The people are left in an appalling state. Everyone can think only of his or her own survival:

Those who died by the sword had it better	טוֹבִים הָיוּ חַלְלֵי־חֶרֶב
than those who died by famine,	מֵחַלְלֵי רָעָב,
and who pined away, stricken	שֶׁהֵם יָזֻבוּ מְדֻקָּרִים
by [lack of the] produce of the fields.	מִתְּנוּבוֹת שָׂדָי.
The hands of compassionate women	יְדֵי נָשִׁים רַחֲמָנִיּוֹת
have cooked their own children,	בִּשְּׁלוּ יַלְדֵיהֶן,
in order to devour them,	הָיוּ לְבָרוֹת לָמוֹ,
at the destruction of the daughter of my people.	בְּשֶׁבֶר בַּת־עַמִּי.

[Lam. 4:9–10]

PRAYER VOCABULARY

sword	חֶרֶב
famine	רָעָב
produce of the fields	תְּנוּבוֹת
women	נָשִׁים

The reaction of Israel's enemies was a combination of joy, exultation, and unbelief:

All who pass by,	סָפְקוּ עָלַיִךְ כַּפַּיִם
they clap their hands over you.	כָּל־עֹבְרֵי דֶרֶךְ.
They hiss and wag their heads	שָׁרְקוּ וַיָּנִעוּ רֹאשָׁם
over the daughter of Jerusalem.	עַל־בַּת יְרוּשָׁלָ͏ִם.
"Is this the city of which it is said	הֲזֹאת הָעִיר שֶׁיֹּאמְרוּ
that she is the perfection of beauty?	כְּלִילַת יֹפִי?
A joy to all the earth?"	מָשׂוֹשׂ לְכָל־הָאָרֶץ?

[Lam 2:15]

The kings of the earth cannot believe,	לֹא הֶאֱמִינוּ מַלְכֵי־אֶרֶץ.
nor can anyone in the world,	כֹל יֹשְׁבֵי תֵבֵל,
that an enemy or a foe could enter	כִּי יָבֹא צַר וְאוֹיֵב
the gates of Jerusalem.	בְּשַׁעֲרֵי יְרוּשָׁלָ͏ִם:

[Lam 4:12]

However, the writer of Eicha knew that the destruction of Jerusalem was not arbitrary. The people had sinned, and the fall of Jerusalem was God's punishment for their sins. The writer knew that the punishment would end within a reasonable amount of time, and that there was hope for the restoration of Israel and the punishment of their enemies in the end.

PRAYER VOCABULARY			
hands	כַּפַּיִם	the world	תֵבֵל
their heads	רֹאשָׁם	the gates of	שַׁעֲרֵי
perfection of beauty	כְּלִילַת יֹפִי		

Your punishment is over, O daughter of
Zion.

תַּם־עֲוֺנֵךְ, בַּת־צִיּוֹן.

He will not continue to keep you in exile.

לֹא יוֹסִיף לְהַגְלוֹתֵךְ.

But your crimes, O daughter of Edom, he
will avenge.

פָּקַד עֲוֺנֵךְ בַּת־אֱדוֹם.

He will uncover your sins.

גִּלָּה עַל־חַטֹּאתָיִךְ.

[Lam 4:22]

Restore us, Adonai,
and we shall be restored.

הֲשִׁיבֵנוּ יְהֹוָה אֵלֶיךָ,
וְנָשׁוּבָה.

Renew our days as of old!

חַדֵּשׁ יָמֵינוּ כְּקֶדֶם.

[Lam 5:21]

PRAYER VOCABULARY	
your punishment	עֲוֺנֵךְ
daughter of Zion	בַּת־צִיּוֹן
to keep you in exile	לְהַגְלוֹתֵךְ
restore us	הֲשִׁיבֵנוּ
and we shall be restored	וְנָשׁוּבָה
renew our days	חַדֵּשׁ יָמֵינוּ

תְּהִלִּים
TEHILLIM
A BOOK OF SONGS:
FOR EVERY OCCASION

THE BIBLE

The first part of the Bible is called the *Torah*. In five books, it tells the story of the Jews from the beginning of the world until the death of Moses, right before the children of Israel entered the holy land.

The second part of the Bible is called the *Nevi'im*, or in English, the Prophets. The first half of the Nevi'im, the *Nevi'im Rishonim* (Former Prophets), comprises what are called the historical books of the Bible. These carry the story of the Jews from the entry into the Land of Israel under the leadership of Joshua to the exile of the Jews from their land during the time of the Babylonians. The second half of the Nevi'im, the *Nevi'im Achronim* (Latter Prophets), comprises the actual prophetic books of the Bible, so called on account of the prophets whose sayings and stories are contained in them.

The third and last part of the Bible is known as the *Ketuvim* (Writings). It consists of eleven books of varying length and contents. Most of the biblical books that you have learned about in this book, for instance the Five Megillot, are a part of the Ketuvim. The first and longest book of this collection is the one named *Tehillim*, or Psalms.

The name Tehillim comes from the Hebrew root הלל , which means "to praise." Other words which come from this root include the name Hillel, the prayer known as Hallel, and the word *Halleluyah,* "praise Adonai." Tehillim itself, then, means "songs of praise." Hence in English we call the book Psalms, which comes from the Greek and Latin name of the book and means about the same thing as the Hebrew.

Tehillim comes closest to being for Jews what Christians refer to as a "hymnal," that is, a book of songs for use in worship. There are 150 psalms in Tehillim, and they can be divided into several categories for use on different types of occasions.

There are songs of lament addressed to God on behalf of both individuals and the community of worshippers as a whole (for another example of this, see Eicha). There are songs of rejoicing and thanksgiving, songs praising the glory and justice of God, and songs in honor of the king as God's faithful servant. Some psalms were meant to be said in private, and some in public, some on the way to the Temple in Jerusalem, and some when returning home.

Because of the varied nature of the psalms, and their religious content, they have served the needs of Jews everywhere for thousands of years in their religious services.

Most of Tehillim was written and recited when the First Temple still stood in Jerusalem. Over the course of the centuries, these psalms were gathered and joined together in the book in which they have come down to us today. The psalms collected in Tehillim are further divided into five smaller collections, or books. These are meant to correspond to the five books of the Torah. Some evidence exists that the number of psalms was originally connected with the number of weekly readings from the Torah, which was once spread out over three years, and not one, as it is now done in most synagogues.

Just as Jewish tradition ascribes the writing of the books of Shir Hashirim, Proverbs, and Kohelet to King Solomon, Jewish tradition ascribes the writing of Tehillim to Solomon's father, King David. There are two reasons for this. First, nearly half of the psalms have the heading לְדָוִד ("of David" or "concerning David"). Second is the very strong evidence in the Bible that David was very famous in his lifetime for his ability in, and love of, music. The classic picture that one has of David is the one of the youthful shepherd playing his harp for King Saul. This image is powerfully preserved in the Twenty-third Psalm.

PSALM 23

This is probably the psalm which is the most familiar to us in the Western world.

THE LORD IS MY SHEPHERD

A song of David:	מִזְמוֹר לְדָוִד:
Adonai is my shepherd,	יְהֹוָה רֹעִי,
I lack nothing.	לֹא אֶחְסָר.
He makes me lie down in green fields,	בִּנְאוֹת דֶּשֶׁא יַרְבִּיצֵנִי,
he leads me to [the banks of] restful	עַל־מֵי מְנֻחוֹת
waters,	יְנַהֲלֵנִי,
he restores my soul.	נַפְשִׁי יְשׁוֹבֵב.

[Ps 23:1–2]

PRAYER VOCABULARY

my shepherd	רֹעִי
in green fields	בִּנְאוֹת דֶּשֶׁא
my soul	נַפְשִׁי

HE LEADS ME

He leads me in the paths of righteousness

    for the sake of his name.

Even were I to walk

    in a valley of darkest shadow,

    I would not fear evil.

For you are with me.

Your rod and your staff comfort me.

יַנְחֵנִי בְמַעְגְּלֵי־צֶדֶק

לְמַעַן שְׁמוֹ.

גַּם כִּי־אֵלֵךְ

בְּגֵיא צַלְמָוֶת,

לֹא־אִירָא רָע.

כִּי־אַתָּה עִמָּדִי.

שִׁבְטְךָ וּמִשְׁעַנְתֶּךָ הֵמָּה יְנַחֲמֻנִי.

[Ps 23:3–4]

MY CUP IS OVERFLOWING

You set a table for me before my foes.

You have salved my head with oil.

My cup is filled to overflowing.

Surely, goodness and lovingkindness will

    pursue me

    all the days of my life.

And I shall dwell in the house of Adonai

    forever.

תַּעֲרֹךְ לְפָנַי שֻׁלְחָן נֶגֶד צֹרְרָי.

דִּשַּׁנְתָּ בַשֶּׁמֶן רֹאשִׁי.

כּוֹסִי רְוָיָה.

אַךְ טוֹב וָחֶסֶד

יִרְדְּפוּנִי

כָּל־יְמֵי חַיָּי.

וְשַׁבְתִּי בְּבֵית־יְהֹוָה

לְאֹרֶךְ יָמִים.

[Ps 23:5–6]

PRAYER VOCABULARY

he leads me	יַנְחֵנִי	my foes	צֹרְרָי
in a valley of darkest shadow	בְּגֵיא צַלְמָוֶת	my head	רֹאשִׁי
with me	עִמָּדִי	will pursue me	יִרְדְּפוּנִי
comfort me	יְנַחֲמֻנִי	forever	לְאֹרֶךְ יָמִים

169

Psalm 23 is an exceptional example of a song of confidence in God, his protection and justice. It is also, even in English translation, an excellent example of what all the psalms ultimately are: great poetry of a sublime religious character.

In the traditional Jewish liturgy, Psalm 23 is recited by a person who is ill, and as part of the burial service. It can be found as part of the memorial, or Yizkor, service.

Although Jewish tradition ascribes the writing of the Book of Psalms to David—and it is very likely that a number of the psalms not only come from his time but were actually written by him—several other people are mentioned in Tehillim as the authors of individual psalms. These include David's son Solomon, Moses, the sons of Korach and the sons of Asaph (both of whom were groups of Temple functionaries), and others.

Only about half of the psalms appear in the traditional prayerbook in their entirety as definite parts of the various worship services. However, all the psalms were used to supply lines and quotation in other prayers which were written throughout the ages. And the whole Book of Psalms appears in some traditional prayerbooks on account of the psalms' inspirational character.

A few of the more famous psalms that appear as a part of one service or another are discussed below.

ASHREI: PSALM 145

Ashrei ("happy") is a psalm that is traditionally recited at both weekday and Shabbat services.

אַשְׁרֵי Ashrei is Psalm 145, with the addition of the first two lines from elsewhere in Tehillim. It is a hymn of praise to God which is written in *acrostic* form, in other words, each verse starts with a different letter of the alphabet.

Happy are they that dwell in your house. אַשְׁרֵי יוֹשְׁבֵי בֵיתֶךָ.

They continually praise you. Selah. עוֹד יְהַלְלוּךָ סֶּלָה.

[Ps 84:5]

Happy is the people in that situation. אַשְׁרֵי הָעָם שֶׁכָּכָה לּוֹ.

Happy is the people whose God is Adonai. אַשְׁרֵי הָעָם שֶׁיהוָה אֱלֹהָיו.

[Ps 144:15]

PRAYER VOCABULARY

| your house | בֵּיתֶךָ |
| happy | אַשְׁרֵי |

Focus on Selah

The meaning of the word *selah* is one of the biggest unsolved mysteries of the Bible. It appears a total of seventy-one times in Tehillim, and another three times elsewhere. Jewish tradition is unclear about the meaning of *selah.* Both the Targum (the translation of the Bible into Aramaic) and the Talmud understood the word as meaning "forever." However, Rabbi David Kimchi, the RaDaK, from southern France, thought that it was an instruction to the worshippers to raise something up, but what? Hands in prayer? Voices in song? Rabbi Abraham ibn Ezra, who was born in Spain and lived from 1089 to 1164, felt that it was a response of the congregation like *amen* (which is a Hebrew word and means "so be it" or "that's the way it is"). Modern scholars, with all their knowledge of ancient languages and literature, have been unable to decide what *selah* means. The most popular guess is that it was some sort of musical notation, originally written in the margin, which crept into the body of the text when it was copied by someone who had forgotten what it meant. What do you think *selah* means?

A psalm of David: תְּהִלָּה לְדָוִד:

PRAISE

Aleph   I will exalt you, my God, the King,   אֲרוֹמִמְךָ אֱלוֹהַי הַמֶּלֶךְ,

    and I will bless your name   וַאֲבָרְכָה שִׁמְךָ

    forever and ever.   לְעוֹלָם וָעֶד.

Bet   Every day I will bless you,   בְּכָל־יוֹם אֲבָרְכֶךָ,

    and I will praise your name   וַאֲהַלְלָה שִׁמְךָ

    forever and ever.   לְעוֹלָם וָעֶד:

Gimel   Great is Adonai   גָּדוֹל יְהֹוָה

    and most praiseworthy,   וּמְהֻלָּל מְאֹד,

    his greatness cannot be fathomed.   וְלִגְדֻלָּתוֹ אֵין חֵקֶר.

[Ps 145:1–3]

Tav   My mouth shall declare the praise   תְּהִלַּת יְהֹוָה יְדַבֶּר פִּי.

    of Adonai.

    Let all flesh bless his holy name for ever   וִיבָרֵךְ כָּל־בָּשָׂר שֵׁם קָדְשׁוֹ

    and ever.   לְעוֹלָם וָעֶד.

[Ps 145:21]

PRAYER VOCABULARY	
I will exalt you	אֲרוֹמִמְךָ
and I will bless you	וַאֲבָרְכָה
I will bless you	אֲבָרְכֶךָ
and I will praise	וַאֲהַלְלָה
his greatness	גְדֻלָּתוֹ
his holy name	שֵׁם קָדְשׁוֹ

172

In the traditional liturgy for the morning service there is a separate special psalm for each day of the week. At the Shabbat evening services, six psalms are recited for the six work days, then Lecha Dodi is sung, after which a special psalm is recited for Shabbat.

PSALM 29

Psalm 29 represents the psalm for the sixth day.

A psalm of David:	מִזְמוֹר לְדָוִד:
Ascribe to Adonai, O divine beings.	הָבוּ לַיהוָֹה בְּנֵי אֵלִים,
ascribe to Adonai glory and might!	הָבוּ לַיהוָֹה כָּבוֹד וָעֹז!
Ascribe to Adonai the glory of his name!	הָבוּ לַיהוָֹה כְּבוֹד שְׁמוֹ!
Worship Adonai in holy grandeur!	הִשְׁתַּחֲווּ לַיהוָֹה בְּהַדְרַת־קֹדֶשׁ!

[Ps 29:1–2]

PRAYER VOCABULARY

glory	כָּבוֹד
and might	וָעֹז
worship	הִשְׁתַּחֲווּ
in holy grandeur	בְּהַדְרַת־קֹדֶשׁ

THE VOICE OF GOD

The voice of Adonai is over the waters;   קוֹל יְהוָה עַל־הַמָּיִם;

The God of glory thunders;   אֵל־הַכָּבוֹד הִרְעִים:

    Adonai is over many waters.   יְהוָה עַל־מַיִם רַבִּים.

The voice of Adonai with power,   קוֹל־יְהוָה בַּכֹּחַ,

    the voice of Adonai with grandeur,   קוֹל יְהוָה בֶּהָדָר,

    the voice of Adonai breaks cedars,   קוֹל יְהוָה שֹׁבֵר אֲרָזִים,

    Adonai shatters the cedars of Lebanon.   וַיְשַׁבֵּר יְהוָה אֶת־אַרְזֵי הַלְּבָנוֹן.

He makes them skip like a calf,   וַיַּרְקִידֵם כְּמוֹ־עֵגֶל ,

    Lebanon and Sirion [Syria] like   לְבָנוֹן וְשִׂרְיוֹן כְּמוֹ

    a young wild-ox.   בֶן־רְאֵמִים.

[Ps 29:3–6]

GOD AND HIS PEOPLE

Adonai will give strength to his people;   יְהוָה עֹז לְעַמּוֹ יִתֵּן;

    Adonai will bless his people with peace.   יְהוָה יְבָרֵךְ אֶת־עַמּוֹ בַשָּׁלוֹם.

[Ps 29:11]

PRAYER VOCABULARY

with power	בַּכֹּחַ	a calf	עֵגֶל
with grandeur	בֶּהָדָר	strength	עֹז
cedars	אֲרָזִים	with peace	בַשָּׁלוֹם
he makes them skip	וַיַּרְקִידֵם		

Focus on B'nai Elim

One characteristic that makes the Psalms so appealing is that they are universal in nature. They are open to all types of interpretations. This is due in part to the fact that they are poems. Another reason that psalms lend themselves to interpretation is that many of them have words whose meanings can only be guessed. An example of this occurs in Psalm 29. the very first verse of this psalm contains the Hebrew phrase "b'nai elim." In this book it is translated as "divine beings." The great Spanish Biblical commentator Abraham Ibn-Ezra (1089-1164) specifically states that these beings are angels. In the midrash on Psalms (Tehillim Rabbah), many other explanations of this phrase are given. One view makes a pun of "elim" and translates it as "ilem," meaning mute. In this case, the verse means that the mute ones (Israel) should speak to God. Another interpretation of "elim" is "rams." According to this view, the verse means that Israel should be ready to act as a sacrifice for God. Still a third opinion is that "elim" means "nobles." In this case the noble ones are taken to be the patriarchs (Abraham, Isaac and Jacob). This explanation is developed in the Midrash. The first prayer of the Amidah concerns the patriarchs (Avot). With this in mind, the midrash goes on to analyze the rest of Psalm 29 fitting each verse which mentions God to one of the 18 benedictions of the Amidah.

PSALM 92

Psalm 92 is the only psalm which specifically relates to Shabbat. It was probably recited on Shabbat by the Levites, who were the singers and musicians in the Temple. This psalm sings the praises of God, who rewards the righteous and punishes the evil.

A psalm, a song for the Sabbath Day: מִזְמוֹר שִׁיר לְיוֹם הַשַּׁבָּת:

PRAISE GOD

It is good to give thanks to Adonai,   טוֹב לְהֹדוֹת לַיהֹוָה

and to sing to your name, O Most High,   וּלְזַמֵּר לְשִׁמְךָ עֶלְיוֹן,

to recount your kindness in the morning,   לְהַגִּיד בַּבֹּקֶר חַסְדֶּךָ,

and your faithfulness at night,   וֶאֱמוּנָתְךָ בַּלֵּילוֹת,

on the lyre, on the harp,   עֲלֵי־עָשׂוֹר וַעֲלֵי־נָבֶל.

and by the melody of the lute.   עֲלֵי הִגָּיוֹן בְּכִנּוֹר.

[Ps 92:1–4]

PRAYER VOCABULARY	
to give thanks	לְהֹדוֹת
and to sing	וּלְזַמֵּר
to recount	לְהַגִּיד
on the lyre	עֲלֵי־עָשׂוֹר
and on the harp	וַעֲלֵי־נָבֶל

The righteous

    shall blossom like the palm tree;

    shall grow like the cedar in Lebanon.

Planted in the house of Adonai,

    in the courts of our God they shall

      bloom.

They shall continue to prosper in old age,

    they shall flourish and be luxuriant.

To recount that Adonai is upright,

    my Rock

    in whom there is no wickedness.

צַדִּיק

כַּתָּמָר יִפְרָח;

כְּאֶרֶז בַּלְּבָנוֹן יִשְׂגֶּה.

שְׁתוּלִים בְּבֵית יְהֹוָה,

בְּחַצְרוֹת אֱלֹהֵינוּ

יַפְרִיחוּ.

עוֹד יְנוּבוּן בְּשֵׂיבָה,

דְּשֵׁנִים וְרַעֲנַנִּים יִהְיוּ.

לְהַגִּיד כִּי־יָשָׁר יְהֹוָה,

צוּרִי

וְלֹא־עַוְלָתָה בּוֹ.

[Ps 92:13–16]

PRAYER VOCABULARY	
cedar	אֶרֶז
courts	חַצְרוֹת
my Rock	צוּרִי

HALLEL: SONGS OF PRAISE

Hallel is a collection of six psalms, numbers 113 through 118, which are read on certain special occasions. These psalms are read on the three pilgrimage festivals of Pesach, Shavuot, and Sukkot, on Chanukah, and on Rosh Chodesh, which is the first day of the month. In Israel, they are also read by some on Independence Day and on Jerusalem Day.

The whole mood of Hallel is one of jubilation and rejoicing. Therefore these psalms are most appropriate for such celebrations.

THE EXODUS

When Israel went out from Egypt,	בְּצֵאת יִשְׂרָאֵל מִמִּצְרָיִם,
the house of Jacob from a foreign people,	בֵּית יַעֲקֹב מֵעַם לֹעֵז,
Judah became his holy place,	הָיְתָה יְהוּדָה לְקָדְשׁוֹ,
Israel his dominion.	יִשְׂרָאֵל מַמְשְׁלוֹתָיו.

TO CANAAN

The sea saw and fled;	הַיָּם רָאָה וַיָּנֹס;
the Jordan turned back.	הַיַּרְדֵּן יִסֹּב לְאָחוֹר.
The mountains skipped like rams,	הֶהָרִים רָקְדוּ כְאֵילִים,
the hills like sheep.	גְּבָעוֹת כִּבְנֵי־צֹאן.
What's wrong with you, O sea, that	מַה־לְּךָ הַיָּם
you flee?	כִּי תָנוּס?
O Jordan, that you turn back?	הַיַּרְדֵּן תִּסֹּב לְאָחוֹר?
O mountains, that you skip like rams?	הֶהָרִים תִּרְקְדוּ כְאֵילִים?
O hills, like sheep?	גְּבָעוֹת כִּבְנֵי־צֹאן?

PRAYER VOCABULARY

his dominion	מַמְשְׁלוֹתָיו	hills	גְּבָעוֹת
the mountains	הֶהָרִים	like sheep	כִּבְנֵי־צֹאן
like rams	כְאֵילִים		

Dance, O earth, before Adonai,	מִלִּפְנֵי אָדוֹן חוּלִי אָרֶץ,
before the God of Jacob,	מִלִּפְנֵי אֱלוֹהַּ יַעֲקֹב
who can turn the rock into a	הַהֹפְכִי הַצּוּר
pool of water,	אֲגַם־מָיִם
the flint into a spring of water.	חַלָּמִישׁ לְמַעְיְנוֹ־מָיִם.

[Ps 114:1–8]

Like Psalm 29, this psalm shows the power of God over all creation. The mythical imagery of mountains skipping and dancing is echoed in that psalm, especially when one realizes that Lebanon and Sirion were originally names of mountains.

GOD'S KINDNESS

Give thanks to Adonai, for he is good.	הוֹדוּ לַיהֹוָה כִּי־טוֹב.
For his kindness endures forever.	כִּי לְעוֹלָם חַסְדּוֹ.
Let Israel say:	יֹאמַר־נָא יִשְׂרָאֵל:
"For his kindness endured forever."	כִּי לְעוֹלָם חַסְדּוֹ.
Let the house of Aaron say:	יֹאמְרוּ־נָא בֵית־אַהֲרֹן:
"For his kindness endures forever."	„כִּי לְעוֹלָם חַסְדּוֹ".
Let those who worship Adonai say:	יֹאמְרוּ־נָא יִרְאֵי יְהֹוָה:
"For his kindness endures forever."	„כִּי לְעוֹלָם חַסְדּוֹ".

[Ps 118:1–4]

PRAYER VOCABULARY

pool of water	אֲגַם־מָיִם
into a spring of water	לְמַעְיְנוֹ־מָיִם
give thanks	הוֹדוּ
his kindness	חַסְדּוֹ

THE PSALMIST

In distress, I called upon Adonai.

Adonai answered me by setting me free.

Adonai is with me, I am not afraid;

    what could anyone do to me?

מִן־הַמֵּצַר קָרָאתִי יָּהּ.

עָנָנִי בַמֶּרְחָב יָהּ.

יְהֹוָה לִי לֹא אִירָא;

מַה־יַּעֲשֶׂה לִי אָדָם?

[Ps 118:5-6]

It is better to seek refuge in Adonai

    than to trust in humankind.

It is better to seek refuge with Adonai

    than to trust in rulers.

טוֹב לַחֲסוֹת בַּיהֹוָה

מִבְּטֹחַ בָּאָדָם.

טוֹב לַחֲסוֹת בַּיהֹוָה

מִבְּטֹחַ בִּנְדִיבִים.

[Ps 118:8–9]

PRAYER VOCABULARY

in distress	מִן־הַמֵּצַר	than to trust	מִבְּטֹחַ
I am not afraid	לֹא אִירָא	in rulers	בִּנְדִיבִים
to seek refuge	לַחֲסוֹת		

These two psalms are paired in Jewish thought and liturgy. Psalm 137 is a sad song of the Babylonian Exile (which would make it hard for David to have written it, since he had been dead for over four hundred years!). After the first Temple was destroyed in 586 B.C.E., a large number of Jews were exiled to Babylon. This is a song which expresses their deep longing for their homeland. (An Italian version of this psalm was set to music by Giuseppe Verdi for one of his operas. It became the anthem of the Italians in their war of independence from Austrian rule in the last century.) Psalm 126 is a song of rejoicing at the return and restoration of the people from exile.

Both of these psalms are associated with the grace after meals, the *Birkat Hamazon*. Psalm 137 is read as an introduction to the Birkat Hamazon during the week, while Psalm 126 introduces it on Shabbats and festivals. In recent years, it has become customary in some circles to include these two psalms in the celebration of Israeli Independence Day, Yom Ha'atzmaut. Why do you think this is done?

By the rivers of Babylon,

   there we sat and wept,

      when we remembered Zion.

There, on the willows,

   we hung our lyres.

For there our captors demanded

   words of song,

   and our oppressors joy:

"Sing us a song of Zion!"

How could we sing a song of Adonai

   on foreign soil?

If I forget you, O Jerusalem,

   may my right hand wither.

May my tongue stick to the roof

   of my mouth,

     if I do not remember you,

     if I do not raise Jerusalem above

      highest joy.

עַל־נַהֲרוֹת בָּבֶל,

שָׁם יָשַׁבְנוּ גַּם־בָּכִינוּ,

בְּזָכְרֵנוּ אֶת־צִיּוֹן.

עַל־עֲרָבִים בְּתוֹכָהּ,

תָּלִינוּ כִּנֹּרוֹתֵינוּ.

כִּי שָׁם שְׁאֵלוּנוּ שׁוֹבֵינוּ

דִּבְרֵי־שִׁיר,

וְתוֹלָלֵינוּ שִׂמְחָה:

"שִׁירוּ לָנוּ מִשִּׁיר צִיּוֹן!"

אֵיךְ נָשִׁיר אֶת־שִׁיר־יְהֹוָה

עַל אַדְמַת נֵכָר?

אִם־אֶשְׁכָּחֵךְ יְרוּשָׁלַָם,

תִּשְׁכַּח יְמִינִי.

תִּדְבַּק לְשׁוֹנִי

לְחִכִּי,

אִם־לֹא אֶזְכְּרֵכִי,

אִם־לֹא אַעֲלֶה אֶת־יְרוּשָׁלַַם

עַל רֹאשׁ שִׂמְחָתִי.

[Ps 137:1–6]

PRAYER VOCABULARY

rivers	נַהֲרוֹת	sing us	שִׁירוּ לָנוּ
we sat	יָשַׁבְנוּ	if I forget you	אִם־אֶשְׁכָּחֵךְ
we wept	בָּכִינוּ	my right hand	יְמִינִי
willows	עֲרָבִים	my tongue	לְשׁוֹנִי
our lyres	כִּנֹּרוֹתֵינוּ	to the roof of mouth	לְחִכִּי

A song of going up [to the Temple in Jerusalem]:	שִׁיר הַמַּעֲלוֹת:
When Adonai restored the exile of Zion, we were like dreamers.	בְּשׁוּב יְהֹוָה אֶת־שִׁיבַת צִיּוֹן, הָיִינוּ כְּחֹלְמִים.
Then our mouths filled with laughter, and our tongues with joyous shouts.	אָז יִמָּלֵא שְׂחוֹק פִּינוּ, וּלְשׁוֹנֵנוּ רִנָּה
Then they said among the nations: "Adonai has done great things for them."	אָז יֹאמְרוּ בַגּוֹיִם: "הִגְדִּיל יְהֹוָה לַעֲשׂוֹת עִם־אֵלֶּה."
Adonai has indeed done great things with us.	הִגְדִּיל יְהֹוָה לַעֲשׂוֹת עִמָּנוּ.
We have become happy.	הָיִינוּ שְׂמֵחִים.
Adonai, restore our fortunes like streams in the Negev [desert].	שׁוּבָה יְהֹוָה אֶת־שְׁבִיתֵנוּ כַּאֲפִיקִים בַּנֶּגֶב.
The ones who sow in tears, will reap in joy.	הַזֹּרְעִים בְּדִמְעָה, בְּרִנָּה יִקְצֹרוּ.
The one who goes out weeping, carrying a bag of seeds, will surely come home in joy, carrying bundles of grain.	הָלוֹךְ יֵלֵךְ וּבָכֹה, נֹשֵׂא מֶשֶׁךְ־הַזָּרַע, בֹּא־יָבֹא בְרִנָּה, נֹשֵׂא אֲלֻמֹּתָיו.

[Ps 126:1–6]

PRAYER VOCABULARY			
the exile of Zion	שִׁיבַת צִיּוֹן	like streams	כַּאֲפִיקִים
like dreamers	כְּחֹלְמִים	bag of seeds	מֶשֶׁךְ־הַזָּרַע
and our tongues	וּלְשׁוֹנֵנוּ	in joy	בְּרִנָּה
our fortunes	שְׁבִיתֵנוּ	bundles of grain	אֲלֻמֹּתָיו

Before the actual morning service begins, it is customary to recite a set of psalms known as Pesukei D'Zimra ("verses of song"). The first, and most important, of these is the Ashrei, which was already discussed. The core group of Pesukei D'Zimra is made up of the last psalms in Tehillim. These psalms all revolve around the word *halleluyah,* which means "Praise God!" They are no more—or less—than exuberant songs of praise to God.

The last psalm in Tehillim, number 150, forms a fittingly joyful conclusion both to Tehillim and to this book.

Praise Adonai!	הַלְלוּיָהּ!
Praise God in his sanctuary!	הַלְלוּ־אֵל בְּקָדְשׁוֹ!
Praise him in his mighty heavens!	הַלְלוּהוּ בִּרְקִיעַ עֻזּוֹ!
Praise him for his mighty acts!	הַלְלוּהוּ בִגְבוּרֹתָיו!
Praise him according to his surpassing greatness!	הַלְלוּהוּ כְּרֹב גֻּדְלוֹ!
Praise him with the blast of the shofar!	הַלְלוּהוּ בְּתֵקַע שׁוֹפָר!
Praise him with lute and lyre!	הַלְלוּהוּ בְּנֵבֶל וְכִנּוֹר!
Praise him with drum and dance!	הַלְלוּהוּ בְּתֹף וּמָחוֹל!
Praise him with stringed instruments and flute!	הַלְלוּהוּ בְּמִנִּים וְעֻגָב!

Praise him with sounding cymbals!

Praise him with crashing cymbals!

Let every soul praise Adonai!

Praise Adonai!

הַלְלוּהוּ בְּצִלְצְלֵי־שָׁמַע!

הַלְלוּהוּ בְּצִלְצְלֵי תְרוּעָה!

כֹּל הַנְּשָׁמָה תְּהַלֵּל יָהּ

הַלְלוּיָהּ!

PRAYER VOCABULARY

praise Adonai	הַלְלוּיָהּ	and lyre	וְכִנּוֹר
in his sanctuary	בְּקָדְשׁוֹ	with drum and dance	בְּתֹף וּמָחוֹל
in the heavens	בִּרְקִיעַ	every soul	כֹּל הַנְּשָׁמָה
for him mighty acts	בִגְבוּרֹתָיו		